A DYNASTY INTERRUPTED

A DYNASTY INTERRUPTED

*The Rise and Fall of the 1980s
Atlanta Braves*

PATRICK MONTGOMERY

BLOOMSBURY ACADEMIC
NEW YORK • LONDON • OXFORD • NEW DELHI • SYDNEY

BLOOMSBURY ACADEMIC
Bloomsbury Publishing Inc, 1359 Broadway, New York, NY 10018, USA
Bloomsbury Publishing Plc, 50 Bedford Square, London, WC1B 3DP, UK
Bloomsbury Publishing Ireland, 29 Earlsfort Terrace, Dublin 2, D02 AY28, Ireland

BLOOMSBURY, BLOOMSBURY ACADEMIC and the
Diana logo are trademarks of Bloomsbury Publishing Plc

First published in the United States of America 2026

Copyright © Patrick Montgomery, 2026

Cover image: © Getty Images Sport/Rich Pilling via Getty Images

All rights reserved. No part of this publication may be: i) reproduced or transmitted in any form, electronic or mechanical, including photocopying, recording or by means of any information storage or retrieval system without prior permission in writing from the publishers; or ii) used or reproduced in any way for the training, development or operation of artificial intelligence (AI) technologies, including generative AI technologies. The rights holders expressly reserve this publication from the text and data mining exception as per Article 4(3) of the Digital Single Market Directive (EU) 2019/790.

Bloomsbury Publishing Inc does not have any control over, or responsibility for, any third-party websites referred to or in this book. All internet addresses given in this book were correct at the time of going to press. The author and publisher regret any inconvenience caused if addresses have changed or sites have ceased to exist, but can accept no responsibility for any such changes.

A catalog record for this book is available from the Library of Congress.

ISBN: HB: 979-8-8818-4256-7
ePDF: 979-8-8818-5448-5
eBook: 979-8-8818-5447-8

Typeset by Integra Software Services Pvt. Ltd.
Printed and bound in the United States of America

For product safety related questions contact productsafety@bloomsbury.com.

To find out more about our authors and books visit www.bloomsbury.com and sign up for our newsletters.

This book is for those interrupted along their way but still able to find the detour just as rewarding.

CONTENTS

Acknowledgments viii

Introduction 1

1   A Proud Franchise 5
2   The Abyss 15
3   The Rise 21
4   Roller Coaster Going Up 39
5   Roller Coaster Going Down 69
6   The Chase 99
7   The 1982 Playoffs 125
8   1983 As the Favorites 145
9   The Impatience of the 1984 Offseason 159
10 The Braves Turn Left 167
11 It Had to Happen 173
12 A Model Franchise 179

Notes 183
Bibliography 187
Index 189
About the Author 192

ACKNOWLEDGMENTS

Thank you to the many individuals, companies, and organizations helping me along the way to making this book a reality. I was fortunate enough to get new interviews and perspectives from players, managers, and baseball executives including Joe Torre, Dale Murphy, Bob Horner, Chris Chambliss, Bobby Wine, Eddie Haas, Brian Sabean, John Schuerholz, and Pat Gillick.

Further assistance and guidance were also provided by the Atlanta Braves.

Thank you to the Rita Rosenkranz Literary Agency, Christen Karniski at Bloomsbury Publishing, and Kate Scheinman for serving as my editor.

Hunting and gathering of baseball statistics, biographical information, historical interviews, and so on, were made possible by the absolutely amazing resources of baseball-reference.com, stathead.com, Sabr.org, and the SABR Research Collection, which contains access to the *Baseball Research Journal*, and SABR Digital Library.

Thank you to Topps Company, Inc. for the courtesy of allowing their images.

The biggest thank you of all is to my beautiful wife, Barbara, for the gifts of grace, patience, and my own creative suite in the house allowing me the freedom to swing away at 3–0 fastballs.

INTRODUCTION

During the 1970s, the Atlanta Braves were not a baseball team on the rise. Other than Henry (Hank) Aaron climbing the all-time home run list, there was little for the fans to be excited about. In 1974, Hank Aaron passed Babe Ruth's record, but after the season, Aaron left the only Major League Baseball franchise he played for during his long National League career to return to Milwaukee and finish out for the American League Brewers.

The 1970s were not kind to the Atlanta Braves.

A few years after leaving Milwaukee and approaching the 1970s, the Braves were doing just fine, winning 93 games and taking the National League West Championship before losing to the "Miracle" New York Mets in the 1969 National League Championship Series. So it was hard to believe that the Atlanta Braves would have only two winning seasons during the next decade, and only two more during the 1980s. The Braves went from 1970 to 1982 without a playoff appearance. Finally, a young team with a returning hero as manager led the 1982 team to the playoffs with the budding superstars of Dale Murphy, hitting 36 home runs, and Bob Horner, slugging 32, leading the Braves to the National League West (NLW) title.

The 1982 Braves led the NL in home runs; with an average age of just 27, the Braves had the youngest lineup in the NL. The arrow was pointing up.

In 1983 and 1984 the Braves managed consecutive second-place finishes in the packed NLW. The 1982–1984 Braves teams had the look of a long-term contender, with a future Hall of Fame manager, perhaps the best player in baseball winning back-to-back MVPs, and a young baseball prodigy third baseman manning the hot corner.

The combination of Dale Murphy and Bob Horner is not often placed alongside the more prominent tandems of Ruth and Gehrig, or Mantle and Maris. But the Murphy-Horner duo was certainly one of the best examples of power in baseball history, and they were the property of the Atlanta Braves.

At 6′4″ and 210 pounds, Dale Murphy looked like Captain America, and he hit like a superhero during Joe Torre's tenure with the Braves, winning MVPs, collecting Gold Gloves, and racking up All-Star Game selections with ease. Bob Horner was not quite as tall at 6′1″ and did not have the Captain America mojo, but he could hit the cover off the ball.

Bob Horner came straight to the Braves on June 16, 1978, never even playing in the minor leagues, and Horner combined with Murphy for 474 home runs (HRs) through the 1986 season. The number 474 is the most HRs by a pair of teammates during that timeframe, and the duo also have the most HRs for the National League (379) during the 1980s.

The team was primed for a long run of wins and hopefully for the World Series.

But suddenly after the 1984 season, Joe Torre, the well-liked manager, was fired and replaced with a rookie manager, who struggled with a 66–96 team, finishing near the bottom of the 1985 National League. There would be more losing to come. The Braves finished the 1980s without another winning season. It was not until 1991 that the Braves finished higher than fifth in the NLW.

Torre ended up doing very well for himself the next time he was paired with a talented core of young superstar players. In 1996 Torre led a young New York Yankees team to their first World Series Championship since 1978 with a victory over his former Atlanta Braves. Three years later, Torre added insult to injury by sweeping the Braves 4–0 for the 1999 World Series title. After losing eight games in a row to Torre and the Yankees during the 1996 and 1999 World Series, it wouldn't be until 2021 that the Braves would make it back to the World Series.

It is not quite the Curse of the Bambino of the Red Sox, or the Cubs Curse of the Billy Goat, but the Torre Jinx left a mark on the Braves. With the 1996 Yankees team, Torre went on to manage the Yankees dynasty, bringing home six AL pennants, and four World Series titles during the next eight years.

Joe Torre led a dynasty for the Yankees, but what if he had not been fired by the Atlanta Braves? Torre brought the 1980s Braves from the bottom to fighting for the top during three straight years, only to be fired and have the Braves sink back into the cellar. What went wrong?

Was a dynasty interrupted?

1

A Proud Franchise

TIMELINE OF THE BRAVES

Throughout their long history, the Braves have been called the:
- Boston Red Stockings (1871–1875)
- Boston Red Caps (1876–1882)
- Boston Beaneaters (1883–1906)
- Boston Doves (1907–1910)
- Boston Rustlers (1911)
- Boston Braves (1912–1935)
- Boston Bees (1936–1940)
- Boston Braves (1941–1952)
- Milwaukee Braves (1953–1965)
- Atlanta Braves (1996–present)

There are plenty of Major League Baseball (MLB) teams that can trace their lineage back to previous centuries. But no franchise can trace their roots back quite like the Atlanta Braves. The story of the Braves began in 1871, as the Boston Red Stockings, playing at the South End Grounds as a charter member of the National Association of Professional Base Ball Players (NAPBBP). Starting with those humble beginnings, the Braves are the oldest continually running professional sports team in the United States.

The Braves have a long and storied history from Boston, to Milwaukee, and then finally to Atlanta, and some of the most accomplished MLB ball players were part of the Braves organization. Amazingly, however, unlike some other historic franchises, the number of Braves World Series titles does not reflect the prestige and fabric of their long history, with younger franchises, like the Yankees and Dodgers, having more World Series titles. Although the player names are old today, they still carry sufficient weight to make even a casual baseball fan take note.

For example, an argument can be made that the most prolific pitcher (Cy Young) and most dominant hitter in baseball history (Babe Ruth) finished their careers with the Braves franchise. How can something like that be topped? How about, the best all-around athlete of the 20th century (Jim Thorpe) was also a Brave.

Just as the name Cy Young is synonymous with pitching excellence, the Braves are known for their pitching dominance as well. The Braves are second with eight Cy Young Awards to the Dodgers who top the MLB with 12 Awards for the franchise. It is only fitting that Cy Young was once part of the great Braves franchise.

Baseball's icon of pitching excellence, Cy Young, ended his career with the Boston Rustlers in 1911. Denton True "Cy" Young was nicknamed "Cy" because his fastball was as devastating as a cyclone. In 1911 and playing for the Boston Rustlers, the 44-year-old Young was the oldest player in baseball. Even at that age, on September 22, 1911, Young had the stamina to throw a 1–0 shutout for his 511th victory and 749th complete game. Cy Young racked up eight Complete Games (CG) in 11 Games Started for the 1911 team. By comparison, the 2024 Braves finished with two CG during the 162-game season. Young's 511 wins, 749 CG, and his 325 losses are all MLB records that are now out of reach for today's hurlers due to changes to the game over the last 150 years and the expectation that a starting pitcher only goes through the batting lineup twice per game and rarely completes the game or even throws more than 200 innings during the regular season. In fact, the way a Complete Game used to be played is now part of baseball lore. During the early 1900s, nearly 90 percent of baseball games were completed by the starter, in comparison to just 0.6 percent of MLB games completed by the starting pitcher in 2024.

As large a shadow as Cy Young still casts across the world of baseball, there is no name as big or hallowed as one that is just one word… Babe.

George Herman Ruth was a man of many monikers including the Great Bambino, the Sultan of Swat, the Colossus of Clout, the Big Bam, and the Behemoth of Bust—and we can agree on the Babe.

By the time Babe Ruth joined the Braves in 1935, he was 40 years old and no longer the dominant force of the game. Now a pale shadow of the Sultan of Swat, the Babe was rounder and slower, but he still could bring interest to a team. The Braves wanted him there to bring in fans, and having been named assistant manager, and vice president for the Braves, the Babe was trying to reach his goal of becoming an MLB manager.

The 1935 season started out with a bang for Babe Ruth. He hit a two-run home run (HR), singled in another, and later scored the fourth run to help bring a 4–2 victory in Boston on Opening Day. The next game was followed up with two hits. But the hot start did not last, and it was not long after the season began that Babe Ruth realized he was not being used for his baseball acumen to assist managing the team or have any influence within organizational decisions. Rather, he was there to bring in the fans. The Babe was struggling into May of the early season and wanted to retire but was asked to play until at least Memorial Day.

Babe Ruth was able to wind the clock back several years on May 25, 1935, to give the National League fans in Pittsburgh a flash of what the American League had seen for many years. Babe Ruth went 4-4 with three HRs, and six runs batted in (RBIs). He became the first player to hit a fair ball completely out of the Pittsburgh Pirates Stadium of Forbes Field.

The Sultan of Swat could have retired that day on a high note, but he had promised the Braves and the teams already planning events around him to complete the current road trip. Babe Ruth retired on June 2 of that year. His six Braves home runs brought his career total to 714, an MLB record that would stand until another Brave would surpass it.

As prolific as Cy Young and Babe Ruth were as baseball players, they were far from the best athletes to ever play for the Braves. That honor goes to perhaps the greatest athlete of the 20th century, one whom many may not even know played for the Braves or even for Major League Baseball.

There is a name perhaps forgotten by many today, but before great all-around athletes like Bo Jackson and Deion Sanders, capable of playing multiple sports and fascinating sport fans, there was perhaps the most talented athlete of all-time and he actually played for the Braves.

Jim Thorpe was a member of the Sac and Fox Nation and was the first Native American to win Olympic Gold for the United States, when he earned the Pentathlon and Decathlon Gold Medals during the 1912 Stockholm Summer Games. Thorpe was also a National Football League (NFL) pioneer, professional basketball player, and a Major League Baseball outfielder. Thorpe is also in the College Football and Pro Football Halls of Fame.

Jim Thorpe's Olympic Medals were quickly taken away, however, once it came out that he had previously been paid for playing in a semiprofessional baseball league several years earlier. The International Olympics Committee (IOC) decided to strip Thorpe of his Olympic Titles and declared him a professional athlete in 1913. That decision led Thorpe to look to MLB, leading to a career with the New York Giants, Cincinnati Reds, and Boston Braves while balancing a professional football career.

Jim Thorpe batted .327 in 60 games for the 1919 Boston Braves. His last appearance in MLB was in 1919, but he continued his pro football career eventually becoming the first president of the NFL. Jim Thorpe had his Olympic Medals restored in 1983, but sadly, this was 30 years after his death.

The team name itself, the Braves, is just one of several the team has known throughout their long baseball journey, with the 1936–1940 name decided by a fan poll. As noted in the box at the start of this chapter, the Atlanta Braves also were known as the Boston Red Stockings (1871–1875), Boston Red Caps (1876–1882), Boston Beaneaters (1883–1906), Boston Doves (1907–1910), Boston Rustlers (1911), Boston Braves (1912–1935), Boston Bees (1936–1940), Boston Braves (1941–1952), Milwaukee Braves (1953–1965), and Atlanta Braves (1996–present). But with all these names, the bottom line is that they are the only Major League Baseball franchises to field a team in every year of professional baseball.

The long journey of approximately 150 years for the team now known as the Atlanta Braves contains interesting strands and layers. For example, on January 20, 1871, the Boston Redstockings became one of nine teams in the National Association of Professional Baseball Players (the forerunner of the National League) and won six of the first eight pennants in the league. The year 1875 was an especially dominant one as they won 26 straight games and went 38–0 at home. The 1890s team captured three more pennants.

By 1912, the team's name first became the Boston Braves, and a pennant with a World Series followed in 1914. But much like the Brooklyn Dodgers and NY Giants, Boston was not big enough to maintain multiple teams along with the Boston Red Sox of the American League. So in 1953, the Boston Braves moved to Milwaukee, the city that previously hosted the Braves AAA Minor League team. Their 82-year run in Boston ended with 4,762 victories for the National League Boston franchise, and if you include the 225 wins from the 1871–1875 Boston Redstockings (which played before the NL was formed), the team's victories totaled 4,988.

With less than a 30-day notice to their fans in Boston and well into 1953 spring training, the Braves suddenly announced they were taking their franchise to Milwaukee starting with the 1953 MLB season. This move for the Braves to become the Major League franchise in Milwaukee was a twisting road of serendipity for the Braves organization with ripple effects across baseball.

The Braves moved to Milwaukee and took over a brand-new stadium that had been slated for their AAA minor league team, the Milwaukee Brewers. With the parent team taking over the new stadium, the Brewers moved to Toledo to take over the stadium that the Mudhens had left a year earlier. The Brewers become the Toledo Sox, winning the American (AAA) Championship in 1953.

In 1950, the City of Milwaukee began to build a stadium designed to attract a major sports franchise like the NFL's Green Bay Packers or MLB's St. Louis Browns. The inside track was to the St. Louis Browns, a franchise that was no stranger to Milwaukee; 50 years earlier, the American League baseball Browns, then known as the Milwaukee Brewers, had left Milwaukee for St. Louis after the 1901 season, becoming known as the St. Louis Browns.

In 1952, the St. Louis Cardinals were on the verge of moving to Texas because the Cardinals held the MLB rights to the territory through their AAA team playing in Houston, but a last-minute bid to keep the team in St. Louis was accepted.

The St. Louis Browns, like the Boston Braves, thought there was not enough room in a city with another MLB team. The Browns applied to relocate back to Milwaukee and into the soon-to-be-finished Milwaukee County Stadium, but the Boston Braves, since they had their AAA team in Milwaukee, was able to block the move in accordance with MLB policy at the time. After turning down an $800,000 Browns offer for the Braves to waive the territory, the Braves in turn applied to move to Milwaukee, and ultimately moved the Brewers to Toledo to replace the Mudhens who previously relocated to Charleston, West Virginia. It was a game of musical chairs with the Braves winning and leaving the Browns in St. Louis in 1953.

However, it turned out alright for the St. Louis Browns as they were able to relocate the next year and become the Baltimore Orioles. I hope you got all that.

Milwaukee County Stadium was the first major league ballpark built with lights and the first to be completely financed by public funds. The Braves were able to attract fans to the new stadium at a level they could not do in Boston, setting a then national record for season attendance during their 1953 inaugural season with 1,826,397 and with room to go up in future seasons. The 1957 World Championship year set a season Braves franchise record for attendance of 2,215,40 that would not be passed for another 35 years.

From the start, the stadium was packed, and winning was happening on the field. The exciting Hank Aaron was making his mark, Eddie Mathews was holding down third base, and Warren Spahn was racking up victories in Milwaukee for the Braves. It was a good time for the Braves.

The Milwaukee Braves won the NL Championship in 1957 and 1958. The 1957 season saw the Braves beat the Yankees in seven games for their first World Series Championship since 1914. Then in 1958, the Yankees flipped the script with the Braves losing in seven games. The 3–1 deficit overcome by the New York Yankees was the first in a best-of-seven by an AL team. The only previous instance was by the NL's Pittsburgh Pirates in 1925.

The Milwaukee Braves knew nothing but winning. In fact, the Braves had a winning record in the National League each season while in Milwaukee. Thirteen in a row! The Milwaukee Braves won 1,146 games during their time there finishing the 1953–1965 seasons with a winning percentage of .563. Hall of Famers like Hank Aaron, Phil Niekro, and Joe Torre started their MLB careers in Milwaukee. The already established future Hall of Famers Warren Spahn and second-year player Eddie Mathews moved with the club from Boston; Del Crandall, an 11-time All-Star for the Milwaukee Braves played catcher; and Joe Adcock held down first base and even hit four home runs during one game in 1954 against four different Brooklyn Dodgers pitchers. It was an exciting time for Braves baseball and the city of Milwaukee.

The Braves were winning on the baseball field, but somewhere along the way the fans stopped showing up as much. For nine straight seasons starting the first year in Milwaukee in 1953 the team had at least 1 million fans per year, often above 2 million per year. But from 1962 through 1965, the team failed to hit the 1 million mark. Why?

The Braves were still winning, but instead of being at or near the top of the standings, they were falling to fifth or sixth each year. The Braves owner at the time was Lou Perini, a sharp businessman, who moved the team from his native Massachusetts to Wisconsin for what he believed would be better long-term opportunities. The first nine seasons rewarded his faith with record attendance numbers, but in 1962 the numbers dipped all the way down to 766,921. The Braves franchise went up for sale after the 1962 season. Perini, who had bought the Braves back in 1945 for $500,000, sold 90 percent of the team to a Chicago-based group led by 34-year-old insurance executive William Bartholomay for $5.5 million.

Bartholomay was not a neophyte to baseball. He was previously a part-owner of the Chicago White Sox, and he knew the power and money a larger city could attract, as well as a wide-open television market and the untapped TV revenue that could be harvested, and he soon began to cast his eye elsewhere.

History tends to repeat itself, even in baseball. Much like Milwaukee did to Boston, Atlanta was hoping to do to Milwaukee. The city of Atlanta wanted to attract professional NFL and MLB teams, and with that in mind, Atlanta-Fulton County Stadium broke ground in April of 1964 without a known client. The stadium was built amazingly fast and was completed the following April. Initially the AL Kansas City Athletics was persuaded to go but was blocked by the AL in 1963. By July of 1964, Atlanta found another team that wanted to come, but Milwaukee—despite the drop in fan attendance—was going to fight to keep their Braves.

The Braves wanted to move on, even as Milwaukee did not want them to go. An injunction by the State of Wisconsin held the Braves in Milwaukee for 1965, with attendance falling even more to 555,000 due to the perceived lack of commitment from the team to the local fans.

At this point, the Braves even went as far as to purchase an Atlanta-based AAA minor league team from the Minnesota Twins and moved them to Atlanta-Fulton County Stadium to secure the Atlanta MLB territory and stadium for themselves.

The first professional baseball game to be played at the Atlanta-Fulton County Stadium was an Exhibition Game between the Milwaukee Braves and their AAA team, the Atlanta Crackers, in April 1965. The Crackers completed the year in the new stadium until the Braves were able to settle the Milwaukee court cases and receive approvals in 1965 to move for the upcoming 1966 season.

It was the first and last season for the Atlanta Crackers at Atlanta-Fulton County Stadium, and the Crackers ended as a baseball team having served the need of the Braves organization.

2

The Abyss

The 1966 Atlanta Braves team had a power-packed slugger lineup capable of easily putting runs across. The Braves paced all of MLB with 207 home runs, 782 runs, and 734 RBIs. The San Francisco Giants placed second with 181 home runs, the Baltimore Orioles at 759 runs, and Pittsburgh Pirates at 715 RBIs. With the average age of the offense at 28.2, and the pitching staff at 28.0, they had a team in what should have been the prime of their careers and poised for serious long-term postseason contention. In fact, the 1966 Atlanta Braves baseball diamond was packed with stars in the lineup:

- A young Joe Torre held down the catching position with 36 home runs and 101 RBIs, while hitting .315.

- Felipe Alou, at 31, played first base turning in the best statistical season of his career. Alou led the NL with what turned out to be his career high of 666 at-bats (AB), 122 runs, 218 hits, and 355 total bases. Alou also displayed power with a career high of 31 home runs and led the team in batting average at .327.

- Eddie Mathews, perhaps one of the best all-around third basemen of all time and Braves franchise hero, stood at third base for his last season playing in a Braves uniform. At age 34, it would be his last season playing full-time. Mathews played the next three years in Houston and Detroit before retiring and being inducted into the Baseball Hall of Fame.

- Rico Carty played left field and batted a robust .326.
- Mack Jones played center field, slugging 23 home runs.
- Hank Aaron played right field, and he led the league with 44 home runs and 127 RBIs. The Hammer was 32 and beginning to see the 500 milestone within his sights. Aaron became the eighth player to reach 500 home runs on July 14, 1968, against Mike McCormick.
- Joe Torre, Felipe Alou, and Hank Aaron made the All-Star Team and earned MVP votes in 1966.
- The pitching staff was not as decorated, but Tony Cloninger led the staff with 257 2/3 innings pitched and 14 wins, following his career high of 24 wins with the 1965 Milwaukee Braves.

The official start to the Braves in Atlanta occurred on April 12, 1966, with 50,671 attendees bearing witness to Tony Cloninger delivering a pitch to Matty Alou of the Pittsburgh Pirates at 8:11 PM.

The Braves lost 3–2 in 13 innings with Cloninger pitching all 13 innings. Future Atlanta Braves manager Joe Torre hit the first official regular-season home run for Atlanta Stadium in the fifth inning to take an early 1–0 lead, and he hit another home run in the bottom of the 13th as the Braves came up short in the last inning to take their first loss in Atlanta Braves history.

The Atlanta Braves were good that year, finishing with 85 wins, but this was only fifth in the National League standings.

Their "Pythagorean winning percentage" had them at 91 wins, which means they were a bit unlucky as a team for the 1966 season. Pythagorean winning percentage is an estimate of a team's winning percentage given their runs scored and runs allowed. This is a tool created by baseball historian Bill James. The "minus six" score the 1966 Braves had—that is, 85 (the Braves actual wins) minus 91 (their Pythagorean winning percentage)—was the worst in the National League that year.

Another amplifying statistic may be how the Braves fared in one-run games (games decided by only one run). The World Series bound Dodgers won 95 games that year, going 34–19 in the one-run games while the Braves won 85 games, going 21–26 in one-run games. The Braves also went 6–12 in extra innings, while the Dodgers went 11–5. The 12 extra inning losses for the Braves were the most in the National League that year.

There was work to be done for the 1967 season, and the Braves proved they could put out a winning team, with an explosive offense. Importantly, the fans noticed and turned out to support their team, and they watched on local TV in Atlanta. The broadcast affiliate of the Braves in Atlanta was WSB-TV, the call sign "WSB," meaning "Welcome South, Brother." It seemed the Braves had found a home; they drew almost 1 million more fans than they had in 1965 in Milwaukee. The 1,539,801 number, however, was only best for sixth place in National League attendance, but it showed that baseball could succeed in the Southeast.

It would not be until after their inaugural 1966 season in Atlanta that the Braves could legitimately call themselves the *Atlanta* Braves. This was because even after they put their anchor down in Atlanta and finished their first season there, they had one remaining hurdle from Wisconsin and Milwaukee. Even as the 1966 season began, it was far from certain that the Braves were going to be allowed to stay in Atlanta.

A case brought in a Wisconsin court beginning during spring season of 1966 resulted in a ruling that the Braves and the National League violated Wisconsin's antitrust statutes. The ruling was that the Braves must return to Milwaukee by May 18, 1966, or Milwaukee had to be granted a franchise through the 1967 MLB expansion.

The National League, the Braves, and all the MLB franchises had too much at stake to have the Braves forced to spend more time in what was seen as a smaller market, with limited broadcast outreach potential. So Bowie Kuhn, a lawyer working for the NL, filed an appeal with the Wisconsin Supreme

Court. This time the ruling was favorable to the Braves: the Circuit Court ruling was set aside, and the State Supreme Court ruled that professional baseball had the authority to control where the teams played. This case was then appealed all the way to the U.S. Supreme Court, which on December 12, 1966, in a 4–3 vote with two abstentions, refused to review the decision of the state court, effectively leaving the Wisconsin Supreme Court's favorable MLB decision in place. The Atlanta Braves were free of Milwaukee and to remain in Atlanta.

Bud Selig, a Milwaukee Braves minority owner, divested his shares of the Braves and was determined to bring baseball back to Milwaukee. To help fill the MLB void, he arranged for several preseason and regular season games to be played in Milwaukee County Stadium during 1968 and 1969. In 1968, Selig entered an agreement to purchase the Chicago White Sox and move that franchise to Milwaukee, but that sale was vetoed by the American League. Chicago was the second largest city with a baseball team and the American League wanted to keep their foothold in that market.

In many ways, however, it all worked out for both Bud Selig and Bowie Kuhn. Selig was able to bring Major League Baseball back to Milwaukee in 1970 after purchasing the bankrupt Seattle Pilots; he also eventually served as MLB commissioner and was inducted into the Baseball Hall of Fame in 2017. Bowie Kuhn became the fifth commissioner of baseball in 1969, and during his tenure, attendance went from 23 million in 1968 to 45.5 million in 1983. Kuhn was also inducted into the Baseball Hall of Fame in 2008.

The Braves were now safely in Atlanta, packing in at least a million fans each year. Atlanta television station WSB-TV was broadcasting select games, filling the needs of the local fans, and reaching as far as parts of Alabama, Tennessee, and South Carolina. But the Atlanta Braves, and perhaps all of baseball, were on the precipice of change.

During the late 1960s, businessman Ted Turner was transitioning from making his fortune in the outdoor billboard business to buying up radio stations. Then in 1969, he sold several radio stations, and the following year he purchased WJRJ-TV. Turner quickly changed the call sign of WJRJ-TV to WTCG (Turner Communications Group), and Turner now had content to fill.

NBC Affiliate WSB-TV had the broadcast rights to the Braves from 1966 until 1972, airing 18–20 games per year. Starting with the 1973 season, Turner's WTCG acquired the rights to the Braves for a total of $600,000, which was for 60 games per year for five years.

The 1973 season was perfect timing for the Braves to be on TV as a 39-year-old Hank Aaron slugged 40 home runs in just 392 at-bats to finish the season at 713 career home runs, just one home run from tying Babe Ruth's record and two from breaking it. Atlanta Stadium had about 800,000 fans that year, only good for the 11th of 12 teams in attendance numbers, but countless fans across the Southeast region who were not located close enough to Atlanta to attend games in person on a regular basis, were now able to tune in to WTCG to watch the Home Run Chase.

Hank Aaron quickly surpassed Babe Ruth in the 1974 season, and that was his last season in Atlanta. Attendance had been steadily declining since the first season high in 1966 of 1.5 million. With Aaron going back to Milwaukee in 1975, the Braves attendance fell all the way to 555,000, which was about the same as 1965 in Milwaukee. The attendance numbers had the Braves and MLB thinking that a mistake had been made in having the Braves move to Atlanta.

Rumors quickly spread of a possible relocation. Ted Turner had managed to syndicate the games and use them on his affiliate stations and sell them to other stations to fill airtime when broadcast shows were on hiatus; Turner relied on the Braves for content and revenue. Turner also held the TV rights to the National Basketball Association's Atlanta Hawks. In 1976, Turner bought the Atlanta Braves for $10 million. The deal was for $1 million down and $1 million for each of the next nine years with interest. And then in 1977, Turner also purchased the Atlanta Hawks.

Ted Turner and WTCG changed the trajectory of the Atlanta Braves and perhaps all of baseball on December 17, 1976, when his company was able to secure an uplink of the station signal to Satcom 1 satellite enabling distribution to cable providers and National Broadcasts beginning with the 1977 season. The Braves were now on their way to becoming America's team, with millions of viewers. By 1979, the station was rebranded WTBS (Turner Broadcasting System) and TBS was born.

The Ted Turner era of the Braves was off to a loud start, and the carnival was coming to town.

3

The Rise

Ted Turner was loud and brash like George Steinbrenner, eager to spend money to win. Turner entertained his audiences like Bill Veeck, Bill Shanahan, and even today's Savannah Banana's Jesse Cole. Ted Turner became a disruptor to baseball, an agitator to the owners, and a pioneer in the TV-era of baseball.

Turner signed pitcher Andy Messersmith as one of the first million-dollar free agents in 1976 and promptly assigned him the number 17 to correspond with WTBS TV 17 even giving Messersmith the nickname of "Channel" sewn on the uniform above the number for maximum exposure. The National League quickly squashed this advertising ploy citing MLB rules at the time that team jerseys were not allowed to incorporate advertisements other than that of the jersey's manufacturer.

Ted Turner continued to thumb his nose at baseball rules, etiquette, and protocol in 1977, riling up MLB and fellow owners.

The early days of free agency—where players had more of a say as to where they were free to play baseball—were reminiscent of the Wild West without clear-cut rules designed to stop tampering. But MLB Commissioner Bowie Kuhn did his best to navigate the process through carefully worded memos designed to ensure the team that held the expiring contract of a player had exclusive negotiating rights before a player could hit the open market. After Ted Turner told Bob Lurie, the San Francisco Giants owner, that Turner was willing to pay whatever it took to get Gary Matthews to sign with the

Braves, however, this story was picked up in the media and appeared in several newspapers.

Turner did just that, signing Matthews to a five-year, $1.875 million contract with the Braves on November 18, 1976. Several months later, on January 2, 1977, Ted Turner was levied a one-year suspension for his actions.

The remarks made to Lurie, the month before at the World Series, were deemed by MLB Commissioner Kuhn to be tampering. In addition to suspending Turner for a year from team operations, an upcoming first round selection would be taken away from the Braves. However, Turner was able to successfully appeal the MLB Draft restriction and had his suspension lifted. The pick turned out to be Bob Horner from Arizona State University, the number 1 overall pick.

After the offseason of turmoil and mostly escaping with his skin intact, Turner couldn't help himself as the team became mired in an early season losing streak. Sixteen straight losses caused Turner to do something an owner had not done in decades: Ted Turner sent his manager, Dave Bristol, on a 10-day hunting trip so that he (Turner) could become the Braves interim manager. Wearing number 27, Turner led his team to a 2–1 loss. That May 11, the Braves went 0–1with their new manager before the National League demanded Turner leave the dugout as manager.

Turner became the first owner/manager in the majors since Connie Mack, back in 1950. Ted Turner appealed to MLB to allow him to continue to manage, but MLB Commissioner Bowie Kuhn denied the appeal based on the MLB rule that a manager is not able to have a financial stake in the team. Kuhn also cited the fact that Turner did not have the qualifications to manage a baseball team, to which Turner said being able to make enough money to buy an MLB team should count. Turner even asked if he could manage a team in the minor leagues to be qualified, and the answer was still no.

Even with the shenanigans going on in this baseball sideshow, the Braves were quietly bringing pieces together that would one day lead to winning baseball for the team.

The players who made up the Braves of the 1980s came together through the MLB draft, trades, and free agency. They were compiled of All-Stars, Cy Young, MVP, Silver Slugger, and Gold Glove winners. The only problem was that some of the players had those accolades before or after their time with the Braves. Baseball is all about timing, and the timing was off for the 1980s Braves. Here are some players who were on those Braves teams.

Len Barker (Starting Pitcher)

Len Barker did not do anything wrong. He was an excellent pitcher before the Atlanta Braves traded for him in 1983 and signed him to a $4.5 million contract. The issue is the Braves knew he had bone chips in his elbow, and they traded two young players who eventually became very good players for different teams.

At 6'5", Barker was a right-handed pitcher who could throw hard and strike out tons of batters. He led the AL in strikeouts in 1980 and 1981, and he racked up 19 wins in 1980.

On May 15, 1981, pitching for the Cleveland Indians, Barker pitched a perfect game against the Toronto Blue Jays. A perfect game is when the pitcher prevents every batter from the opposing team from getting to first base. This was just the 10th perfect game in Major League Baseball history. Barker had such great control that he never even had a 3-ball count to pitch to. Barker earned his only All-Star selection in 1981 and pitched two scoreless innings in the Cleveland Indians hosted All-Star Game.

His dominance of the last few years began to unravel at the worst time for Len Barker. In 1983 his current contract, and negotiations for a new contract were not going well. On the field, Barker began to suffer from a bone spur that was impacting his powerful fastball and leading to a poor 5.11 ERA across 149 2/3 innings pitched.

But a faltering Barker still carried the glitter of a big name for the TBS Braves during a tough NL West playoff run. The Atlanta Braves believed the arm trouble to be navigable, and on August 28, 1983, they traded three players to be named later and $150,000 for Barker, signing him to a five-year, $4.5 million contract.

For Barker, he was going from the doldrums of playing for a cellar dweller to pitching for a multiyear contract. "I couldn't be happier," said Barker to the *Cleveland Plain Dealer* newspaper at the time of the trade. "I'm going to a first-place team. I got a five-year contract. Wouldn't you be happy to leave a last-place club?"

The late-season acquisition did not work for the Braves, however, as Barker went 1–3 in six starts with the Braves losing the NL West to the Dodgers by a three-game gap.

The Braves doctors had believed the arm issue would be behind Barker, and the Braves sent away the first of the players to be named later, Rick Behenna, on September 2, 1983.

Twenty-three-year-old Rick Behenna was a promising starting pitcher for the Braves in the minor leagues, and in retrospect, he was a fair trade by himself for acquiring Barker for the roughly one month of Barker and his 1–3 record down the stretch and of course the rights to sign Behenna to a long-term multimillion-dollar contract. But the Braves then threw one bad decision after another by making compounded decisions to meter out young future All-Star players in the trade. Brett Butler and Brook Jacoby went to the Indians on October 23, 1983, and capped what may turn out to be the worst trade in Atlanta Braves history.

The bone spurs led to surgery for Barker in 1984, resulting in him missing the last two months of the season and other times in 1985 as well. Len Barker was a combined 9–17, with over 200 innings pitched (IP) for the 1984 and 1985 seasons. He was released during spring training in 1986, leaving the Braves on the hook for the three years remaining on one of the most lucrative pitching contracts at the time. Barker spent 1986 in the minor leagues with the Montreal Expos, finishing his career at age 31 with the Milwaukee Brewers.

Steve Bedrosian (Relief Pitcher)

Steve Bedrosian was drafted by the Atlanta Braves in the third round of the 1978 MLB Draft. He climbed quickly through the minor leagues and made his major league debut in 1981 with 24 1/3 innings in 15 games for the Braves.

Bedrosian was integral to the 1982 Braves as he pitched magnificently mostly out of the bullpen with an 8–6 record, 2.42 ERA, in 64 games, and 137.2 IP. Although he pitched most of his games as a reliever, his 4.2 wins above replacement (WAR) led all the Braves pitchers and was second on the team only to Dale Murphy.

Bedrosian did well in the 1982 accolades earning a 1982 NL Sporting News Rookie of the Year, a spot on the Baseball Digest Rookie All-Star Team, and placing seventh in the NL Rookie of the Year voting. His 4.2 WAR led all National League rookies, and placed second to all Major League Rookies after Cal Ripken Jr.

Bedrosian appeared in a combined 110 games for the 1983 and 1984 Braves with five games started. The Braves decided to switch Bedrosian from a key cog in the bullpen to a spot in the starting rotation for the 1985 season. He had last been a full-time starting pitcher in the minor leagues, but he performed admirably with 7–15 record, putting up 3.83 ERA across 206.2 IP and led the Braves pitching staff with 134 strikeouts. Bedrosian's 37 games started were the fourth most in the National League and second on the Braves to his teammate Rick Mahler who had 39 to lead all of baseball.

Bedrosian was traded by the Braves to the Philadelphia Phillies on December 10, 1985, along with Milt Thompson for Ozzie Virgil and Pete Smith. Virgil did supply big power for the Braves as a catcher in 1987, hitting 27 home runs and earning a spot on the NL All-Star Team.

The Phillies promptly placed Bedrosian back in to the bullpen, where he quickly became one of the best closers in the National League with 29 saves for the Phillies in 1986, before having a career year in 1987 with a 2.83 ERA, and leading Major League Baseball with 40 saves. Bedrossian's dream season included making the All-Star Team and earning the National League Cy Young Award.

Bedrosian played for the Phillies, Giants, and Twins for the 1986–1991 seasons. He played on the 1989 San Francisco World Series team and won a World Championship ring as a member of the 1991 Minnesota Twins. He faced the Braves in three games, all of which happened to be in Atlanta, as the Twins defeated the Braves in seven games to win the World Series.

Bedrosian again signed with the Braves in 1993, slinging a career best 1.63 ERA across 49 2/3 innings. He threw his last major league pitch on August 9, 1995, while he was a member of the Braves. Steve Bedrosian is the only member of the 1982 team to receive a 1995 World Series ring.

Bruce Benedict (Catcher)

Bruce Benedict was a Braves fifth-round pick in the 1976 MLB Draft out of the University of Nebraska at Omaha. Benedict made his MLB debut in August of 1978. His whole MLB career was with the Braves and as catcher. A two-time All-Star, Benedict gave the Braves the luxury of moving Dale Murphy to the outfield. A defensive wizard behind the plate, Benedict set an MLB record by throwing out runners for all three outs of an inning, And Benedict led NL catchers in 1993 with a .993 fielding percentage.

Brett Butler (Outfield)

Brett Butler turned out to be a bargain of a draft pick, but ultimately, he didn't return fair value in a trade for the Braves with his career taking off for other teams.

Drafted by the Atlanta Braves in the twenty-third round of the 1979 MLB June Amateur Draft from Southeastern Oklahoma State University, Butler made his MLB debut two years later with 40 games for the parent club in 1981. In 1982 he was able to play 89 games and provided a spark on the basepaths with 21 stolen bases. His only full season with the Braves was 1983, hitting 5 home runs, 37 RBIs, and batting .281 while playing left field. Butler led the National League with 13 triples and stole 39 bases. He was sent to the Cleveland Indians in the trade for Len Barker after the 1983 season. Brett Butler went on to become an All-Star player with 2,375 hits and batting .290 across 17 MLB seasons. Butler became key as a center fielder for the Indians, Giants, Dodgers, and Mets. He had 100 or more runs six times, leading the NL twice, and he led the NL in triples four times and once in hits.

Rick Camp (Relief Pitcher/Starting Pitcher)

The Atlanta Braves selected Rick Camp in the seventh round of the 1974 June Amateur Draft; he made his debut in 1979 for the Braves as a reliever. From 1976 to 1981, Camp primarily pitched out of the bullpen until transitioning into the starting pitcher rotation in 1982.

Camp was among the NL best relievers for 1980–1981. His ERA for 1980 was a microscopic 1.91, followed up with an even better ERA the following year with 1.78. Rick Camp also placed in the top five in the NL in saves for 1980 and 1981. His dominant 1981 season was highlighted by winning the NL August Pitcher of the Month Award and placing 20th in the MVP voting.

Camp was converted from a reliever to a starting pitcher in June of 1982. He made 21 starts for the team. He proved to be an essential cog in the pitching staff with his 11 wins for the year, tying him for second on the team and his 177.1 IP placing him third. Camp placed 3rd on the staff with his 51 games pitched. Camp found himself on the mound 21 times to start the game and served as the Braves last pitcher 20 times as a reliever.

Camp provided a well-remembered piece of levity to an otherwise dismal Braves team in 1985. He was not a good batter, even by a pitcher's standard, and in his 12 years in professional baseball, he had not hit a home run. But on July 4, 1985, Camp hit a home run against the New York Mets to tie in the 18th inning. In the 19th inning, however, he reverted to form by striking out to end the game and becoming the losing pitcher of the game that started at 7:05 PM on July 4 and—because of three rain delays and extra innings—ended at 3:55 AM on July 5 The Atlanta fans had been promised 4th of July fireworks, and the team delivered them on the 5th of July at 4:00 AM. Not surprisingly the fireworks led to complaints by some residents. Camp finished his career at the end of 1986 Braves spring training after his release by the Braves.

Chris Chambliss (First Base)

Leading up to the 1980 season, the Atlanta Braves acquired Chris Chambliss from the Toronto Blue Jays along with Luis Gomez, in exchange for Barry Bonnell, Joey McLaughlin, and Pat Rockett. The package given for Chambliss was hefty, as McLaughlin was a second-round pick from the 1974 MLB draft, and Rockett was their first-round pick, 10th overall, from the 1973 MLB draft. Luis Gomez did not work out well for the Braves, however, as he batted .192 in approximately 300 at-bats during 1980–1981; Chris Chambliss, however, solidified the Braves infield and provided veteran leadership to the young team. The 1971 American League Rookie of the Year, 1976 All-Star, and 1978 Gold Glove first baseman played for the Atlanta Braves through the 1986 season.

Gene Garber (Relief Pitcher)

On June 15, 1978, Gene Garber was traded to the Braves from the Philadelphia Phillies for Dick Ruthven. Ruthven had demanded to be traded from the Braves when he thought that team owner Ted Turner was being flirtatious with Ruthven's wife. The trade worked out well for both teams the rest of the season; Ruthven went 13–5 for the NL East winning team, and Garber saved 23 games with a 2.53 ERA for the last-place Atlanta Braves. Ruthven earned a World Series ring in 1980 for the Phillies and made the 1981 National League All-Star Team.

By the time Gene Garber was on the Atlanta Braves, he was already a nine-year MLB veteran. One of the highlights of his 1978 season was facing his former Phillies team six weeks after being traded and ending Pete Rose's 44 game hitting streak by striking Rose out in the ninth inning.

Garber had his best season in 1982 helping the Braves to the NL West Championship by saving 30 games, in 69 appearances, with a 2.34 ERA. Garber finished seventh in the 1982 National League Cy Young voting and 19th in the NL MVP voting.

Garber pitched in the Braves bullpen until 1987 with a 3.34 ERA. His 141 saves with the Braves rank third on their all-time list, behind Craig Kimbrel and John Smoltz. With 557 games pitched as a Brave, Garber places fifth behind Phil Niekro's 740 games. Garber was traded in 1987 to the Kansas City Royals and retired the next year.

Bob Horner (Third Base)

Bob Horner was the first pick overall of the 1978 MLB draft going directly from Arizona State to the Major Leagues, making his MLB debut that June. Horner, a two-time NCAA All-American at second base, made the move to third base for the Braves. He earned the National League Rookie of the Year Award in 1978 after hitting 23 home runs and 63 RBIs in just 89 games. Horner was the third baseman from 1978 to 1985, and the full-time first baseman in 1986. Bob Horner earned an All-Star selection in 1982 and hit four home runs in a game in 1986.

Glenn Hubbard (Second Base)

Glenn Hubbard was an Atlanta Braves 20th-round draft pick out of high school in 1975. He made his Braves debut in 1978 and was the Braves second baseman through the 1987 season. Hubbard flourished under Joe Torre, highlighted by his only All-Star Game selection, with career highs of 12 home runs, and 70 RBIs. Hubbard was an excellent fielder, placing in the top five for National League second baseman in assists for seven years, and he was in the top three in Range Factor/Game (Putouts + Assists per Game) each year of his Braves tenure.

Brook Jacoby (Third Base)

Brook Jacoby was a seventh-rounder for the Braves in the 1979 MLB January Draft-Regular Phase and made his MLB debut in 1981. He only had 18 MLB at-bats combined for the 1981 and 1983 seasons. Jacoby was blocked at third base by Bob Horner at the MLB level, but had dominating offensive seasons in the minor leagues highlighted by his 1983 stat line of 25 home runs, 100 RBIs, and a .315 batting average in under 500 at-bats for AAA Richmond.

Brook Jacoby is part of a legacy of perhaps the worst trade in Atlanta Braves history. He and Brett Butler were players to be named later for an August 28, 1983, trade to acquire veteran pitcher Len Barker from the Cleveland Indians, in hopes of a playoff berth. The Atlanta Braves sent Brett

Butler, Brook Jacoby, Rick Behenna, and $150,000 to Cleveland to complete the deal in October of 1983. Jacoby went on to become a two-time All-Star third baseman and was named one of the top-100 All-Time Cleveland Indians players.

Rick Mahler (Starting Pitcher)

The Atlanta Braves signed Rick Mahler as an amateur free agent in 1975, and he made his MLB debut in 1979. Mahler was hardly used for 1979 and 1980 before breaking through to start 14 games and finishing the 1981 season with a 2.80 ERA over 112 1/3 innings. In 1985, he won a career high 17 games. Mahler regularly started 30 games or more for his Braves career through 1988. Mahler signed with the Astros in 1989, and he played briefly for the Expos in 1991 before being released.

Then on June 14, 1991, the Braves again signed Mahler. He managed to pitch in 13 games, with two starts and 28 2/3 IP before being released that August. Mahler is the only member of the 1982 NL West winning team to be on the 1991 NL East and NL Champion Atlanta Braves team.

Craig McMurtry (Starting Pitcher)

In my last book, *Baseball's Great Expectations*, I wrote about players like McMurtry: players who have all the talent, the results in the minor leagues, and yet somehow do not live up to the expectations bestowed upon them.

The Braves took McMurtry in the first round (4th) of the 1980 MLB January Draft-Regular Phase from McLennan Community College (Waco, Texas). The Braves fast-tracked the 20-year-old bypassing the lower rungs of the minors and placing him directly into the Southern League AA Savannah team. McMurtry quickly justified the trust the Braves had in him by returning dominant seasons with a combined 39 wins and 24 losses. He steadily went from 13 games started at AA in 1980 to 32 games started at AAA for the Richmond team. His 1982 season was capped off by earning the International League Pitcher of the Year award.

The 1982 NL West winning Braves team brought the 23-year-old pitching stud to Atlanta for 1983, and McMurtry did not disappoint. He was one of the best pitchers in the NL in 1983, making 35 starts, winning 15 games to just 9 losses, with a 3.08 ERA over 224.2 IP. Craig McMurtry teamed up with Pascual Perez to form a young, strong "top of the rotation" for what turned out to be the last full season for the 44-year-old Niekro as a Brave.

In 1983, Craig McMurtry tied for the lead with 15 wins, and he led the starters in ERA and IP. He placed seventh for the NL Cy Young Award, and he placed second to the Mets Darryl Strawberry in the NL Rookie of the Year Award; McMurtry was named Rookie of the Year by Baseball Digest, and he earned a Sporting News Rookie of the Year. This would be the third time an Atlanta Brave won a Sporting News Rookie of the Year in six years with Bob Horner in 1978 and Steve Bedrosian in 1982. However, McMurtry was not able to follow up his stellar 1983 campaign, and he hit a "rookie wall" in 1984, going 9–17 with a 4.32 ERA over 183 1/3 innings. As a Brave, he only started in 11 more games and appeared in 43 games as a reliever.

On June 4, 1986, McMurtry had the misfortune of allowing a Barry Bonds opposite field home run. Bonds's home run was his first career home run, leading to his eventual 762 that would break Hank Aaron's career home run record of 755.

McMurtry was traded on February 2, 1987, to the Toronto Blue Jays for Dámaso García and Luis Leal. McMurtry never played for the Blue Jays at the MLB level, instead being assigned to their minor leagues before being released during the 1987 off season. McMurtry played for four other team organizations before his retirement in 1995.

Donnie Moore (Relief Pitcher/Closing Pitcher)

The Braves traded away minor league pitcher Dan Morogiello to the St. Louis Cardinals for relief pitcher Donnie Moore on February 1, 1982. Moore had spent his career to that point with the Chicago Cubs, Milwaukee Brewers, and St. Louis Cardinals with mixed results between the major and minor league levels. The 28-year-old went to the Braves and began to turn his career around. In 1982, he appeared in 36 games at AAA Richmond with a sparkling 2.29 ERA across 55 IP.

The 1982 Braves saw enough from Moore on their Richmond team that they called him up in August during the heat of the playoff chase, where he appeared in 16 games down the stretch run, including two games in the NLCS.

Moore continued to be an important part of the Braves bullpen by appearing in 43 games for the Braves and compiling a respectable 3.67 ERA with six saves. But he really began to emerge as one of the top relievers in the National League in 1984, as he stepped into the role of a closing pitcher for the first time.

Donnie Moore appeared in 47 games, with a 4–5 record with a 2.94 ERA. He placed eighth in the National League with 16 saves. Moore was looking for a raise from his 1984 salary of $130,000 and asked for $490,000 for the 1985 season or a longer-term contract. The Braves countered with a huge raise to $375,000, but the Braves and Moore could not agree, and they were scheduled to have an arbitration hearing.

To complicate things further, the Braves signed Bruce Sutter to a six-year $10 million contract to be the Braves top reliever. Ted Turner was a pioneer of deferred major league salaries, now a major league norm with teams like the Dodgers. Sutter's six-year contract paid him $4.8 million and placed another $4.8 million into a deferred payment account at 13 percent interest. Sutter would receive an estimated $1.3 million per year for 30 years after the initial six seasons of the contract.

Up to that point, Sutter was one of the top players in all of baseball and a perennial All-Star, already having won the Cy Young Award and five top-10 finishes in the MVP voting. Sutter's 45 saves in 1984 were a career high and tied Dan Quisenberry for the MLB record (since broken) for saves.

Even if the Braves lost their arbitration case to Moore and had to pay $490,000, it would have been a plus for the Braves compared to Sutter and his $1,354,167 salary for 1985. But the closing role was now full, and Moore was no longer as important in the eyes of the Braves.

Donnie Moore was selected from the Braves as compensation for the Angels' loss of "Type A" free agent Fred Lynn. Because the Angels lost the highest level of player to free agency, they received a pick from the pool of non-protected players. What constitutes a Type A free agent had been determined by the Collective Bargaining Agreement as someone in the top 20 percent of all players in baseball based on the previous two seasons. The Braves were allowed to protect only 24 of their players on their 40-man roster (instead of 26 players) because they had signed Type A free agent Bruce Sutter. Losing Moore was something the Braves did not want, but it was perceived as being less of a hit due to bringing on Sutter.

"We hated to lose him [Moore], but the way things worked out, we were unable to include Donnie on our list of 24 protected players," said Braves general manager John Mullen in a UPI article that January. "With Sutter coming in, we should be alright."

The Braves, however, did not turn out to be alright with Sutter in 1985, instead of Moore. Bruce Sutter ended up saving only 23 games with an inflated 4.48 ERA. For the Angels, Moore ended up bringing in 31 saves, with a miniscule 1.92 ERA as an All-Star, placing seventh in the Cy Young Award, and sixth in the AL MVP voting. He also proved to be a value at pitching for $407,000 for the year.

Donnie Moore pitched well for the Angels in 1986 with a 2.97 ERA, but as he admitted later, he was pitching while injured in the American League Championship Series. With Moore and the Angels needing just one more strike to win the ALCS earning their first trip to the World Series, Red Sox Dave Henderson hit a home run. The Red Sox went on to win the game in extra innings and won Games 6 and 7 to win the American League Pennant facing and losing the 1986 World Series to the New York Mets.

Moore spent 1987 and 1988 battling injuries and was released by the Angels in 1988. He signed with the Royals as a free agent in 1989 but was released that June while in the minor leagues still trying to make it back to the majors. Then on July 18, 1989, Moore ended his own life after wounding his girlfriend with gunfire.

Dale Murphy (Outfield)

Dale Murphy was selected in the first round of the 1974 MLB draft by the Atlanta Braves as the fifth pick. Murphy is one of the greatest players to play for the Braves. He is a seven-time All-Star, back-to-back MVP, has five Gold Gloves as an outfielder, his number is retired, and he is a member of the Braves Hall of Fame. Murphy was drafted during Hank Aaron's last year as a Brave, and Murphy was traded the same year as the Braves drafted Chipper Jones.

Phil Niekro (Starting Pitcher)

Phil Niekro was signed as an amateur free agent in July of 1958 by the Milwaukee Braves. He made his debut at the age of 25 for the Braves in 1964. Niekro pitched out of the bullpen until he was able to start 20 games for the Atlanta Braves in 1967, pitching 207 innings, and leading the NL in earned run average (ERA) at 1.87. His 207 innings pitched (IP) in 1967 were the least he would achieve until 1981. Perhaps the greatest knuckleball pitcher of all time, Niekro led the NL in IP four times during his career with each over

300 IP and his total of 5,404.3 IP is the most by any pitcher in the post-1920 live-ball era.

Niekro won 318 games over his 24-year career, 268 of which were over his 21 years with the Braves. At age 43, Niekro was the Ace of the 1982 Division Winning Braves with a 17-4 record and 225 strikeouts. Niekro was an All-Star, Gold Glove winner, and placed fifth in the Cy Young Award voting.

A five-time All-Star, Niekro won 20 games three times, he was elected to the Braves Hall of Fame with his number 35 retired, and he was inducted into the Baseball Hall of Fame in Cooperstown in 1997. His knuckleball tumbled all the way until his last MLB game in 1987 as a 48-year-old starting one last game for the Atlanta Braves.

Pascual Perez (Starting Pitcher)

The Atlanta Braves acquired Pascual Perez on June 30, 1982, from the Pittsburgh Pirates for Larry McReynolds. Perez started 11 games during the stretch run compiling a 3.06 ERA. Perez went 29-16 over 1983-1984, becoming perhaps the best Braves starter, and earning an All-Star selection in 1983. However, the wheels came off the Braves bus in 1985 as they went 66-96 without Joe Torre as the manager; Torre had been replaced after the 1984 season. Pascual Perez followed suit with a dismal 1-13 record and a 6.14 ERA over 95.1 IP.

Perez was released at the end of spring training in 1986, but perhaps patience was needed by the Atlanta Braves because in 1987, Perez signed with the Montreal Expos and had a career resurgence with several excellent seasons with the Expos and also the Yankees to finish his 11-year career. Perez's 2.44 ERA and 131 strikeouts would have led the Braves pitchers in 1988. With his 1989 pitching line of 12 wins and 3.31 ERA with 152 strikeouts, he would have placed number two, between Hall of Fame pitchers John Smoltz and Tom

Glavine (tied for second in IP, ERA, and strikeouts). Tom Glavine made his Braves debut in 1987 and Smoltz in 1988.

Rafael Ramirez (Shortstop)

Rafael Ramirez signed as an amateur free agent in 1976 out of the Dominican Republic and made his Braves debut in 1980. He played shortstop for the Braves through the 1987 season. Ramirez was an All-Star selection in 1984, after being third in the National League in hits and placing 16th in the NL MVP race. Ramirez led NL shortstops in double plays from 1982 to 1985.

Bruce Sutter (Relief Pitcher)

Bruce Sutter came to the Braves in 1985 as one of the best relief pitchers of all-time. But then Sutter developed shoulder injuries with the Braves, and he played on and off into 1988 ending his Braves career with a 4.55 ERA. Sutter was inducted into the Major League Baseball Hall of Fame in 2006; he is the only pitcher to be in the Hall of Fame without ever starting a Major League game.

✳✳✳

Good Braves players were gathered and ready in 1982:

- Dale Murphy and Bob Horner were locking in as a historic power-tandem,
- Phil Niekro could still make a baseball defy gravity,
- Veteran warhorse first baseman-tandem Chris Chambliss and Bob Watson were ready to show the youngsters how to win, and

- Future Hall of Fame manager Joe Torre was about to take the helm from Bobby Cox, another future Hall of Fame manager.

The Braves went 131–136–1 during 1980–1981. The pieces were all coming together for a Braves team to turn the corner and become a contending team in 1982 and beyond. What could go wrong on the way to greatness? At first everything went right, then everything went wrong, and then perhaps the stirrings of a dynasty team were smothered in the embers waiting to be reignited.

4

Roller Coaster Going Up

The Atlanta Braves began 1982 spring training under Joe Torre expecting to win. During one of his first meetings with the players, he told the team they should be going out on the field with the goal to win a pennant. Team owner Ted Turner put on even more pressure as he proclaimed the Braves "America's Team." But the Braves had to first get through the 1981 World Series Championship-winning Dodgers. Many baseball experts were forecasting a back-of-the-division finish for Torre and the Braves, and why not? Joe Torre was not yet a proven winner.

Joe Torre had only gone 286–420 as the New York Mets manager with a shoddy .405 winning percentage. But he was media savvy, a Braves franchise legend, and he could enjoy the spotlight—so all things required to put on a good show were in place for the Atlanta Braves. Torre showed this early, albeit during spring training, by going 18–6, and the players started to understand what winning consistently felt like. Everyone hoped this success would carry into the season.

After Hank Aaron left the Braves, the years 1975–1979 were a dark time for the team as they would average 95 losses each year. But 1980 produced a winning team with an 81–80 record. The 1981 season was shortened—split into two sections because of the baseball strike—and resulted in a 50–56 season for the Braves, who were not in the playoffs. The 1982 18–6 spring season record meant nothing, and with seven rookies on the Braves Opening Day roster, even the most loyal of Braves fans couldn't have foreseen what was to come.

The 1982 Braves season began April 6 on the road in San Diego against the Padres. Rick Mahler was the unlikely Braves starter as Phil Niekro made his first career trip to the disabled list (now known as the injury list) vacating the Opening Day starter honors for Mahler to pitch against Juan Eichelberger. The starters each put up scoreless innings until the top of the fifth put up the only run to be scored the entire game by either team. A one-out walk to Brett Butler was promptly followed by a double to left field by Glenn Hubbard to score and put the Braves up 1–0.

The 1–0 score for the Braves stood for the win, as Mahler threw a two-hit shutout to take the first game of 1982 for the Braves, who were off and running into the record books.

The Braves took the first two games on the road against the Padres; going home they swept the Houston Astros for three more, and then three more against the Cincinnati Reds. The Braves were now up to eight games and looked like they might have a chance at the modern-day record of 11 wins set by the Oakland As in 1981. The Braves took their winning streak on the road into Houston to beat the Astros for three games to make it 11 consecutive games and tie the modern-day (after 1900) record. The 11th victory was a tight 6–5 battle with Biff Pocoroba doubling to drive in Chris Chambliss and Rafael Ramirez in the top of the eighth, and Rick Camp shut down the Astros in the eighth and ninth innings for the historic win.

With the modern-day record matched, the Braves were primed to go home to Atlanta to battle the Reds to set the modern-day and all-time records.

The fans couldn't wait for the Braves to get to the field to congratulate them on their winning ways. Most of the Braves' winning so far had been on the road, with eight of their first 11 wins in front of hostile crowds. Now the Braves could go for the record at home within the friendly confines of Atlanta-Fulton County Stadium. Even years later, Bob Horner remembers the excitement of the Atlanta Braves fans at the winning streak. "They showed up at the airport, hundreds of them, to greet us as we came home from the road trip. They never did that before, it was great, after so many years of not winning I think we were all of us excited to finally be winning, it was coming together," explained Bob Horner.

The Reds were still a proud team and were lining up to be tough competition for the Braves to go through for possession of the record. The Reds were fresh off winning the NL West in 1981, going 66–42 with a .611 winning percentage in the overall standings. But as the season was split into half, the Reds finished second in each half to place out of the playoffs entirely. The Big Red Machine was less powerful than years past, but they still had Dave Concepcion coming off of 1981's top-five MVP voting, Hall of Famer Johnny Bench, and Tom Seaver with a 14–2 season and second-place finish for the Cy Young Award.

The Braves were down early as Tommy Boggs gave up two runs in the second inning, but the Braves had a Chris Chambliss home run in the bottom of the second, followed by another home run by Rafael Ramirez in the third. Then Claudell Washington smashed a triple to score Glenn Hubbard, and Washington then scored on a wild pitch to give the Braves all the runs they needed in the 4–2 victory. Gene Garber came in for his third save of the year, for the Braves 12th season opening victory, and to set the modern-day record (after 1900) and tie the all-time record that had been set by the 1884 New York Giants.

It was now up to the pitcher who started the Braves with their first victory of the season to win game 13. Rick Mahler was facing Mario Soto to set the all-time record. Many fans may have forgotten how dominant Mario Soto was for the Reds. He pitched in the major leagues for 12 years, all with the Reds, placed in the top-10 of Cy Young Award voting four times, and was named to three All-Star teams. He was arguably his most dominating in 1982, his first of three consecutive All-Star years.

Mahler and Soto were each shutting down the opponent until the Reds broke through with two outs in the top of the third. Larry Biittner, the Reds outfielder who only hit two home runs in 1982, tagged Mahler with a three-run home run to right field placing the Reds in front for a 3-0 lead.

Chris Chambliss hit his third home run of the young season in the top of the fifth inning against Mario Soto to close the gap to a 3-1 Reds lead.

A double to Dale Murphy and a walk to Bruce Benedict finally took Mario Soto out of the game for reliever Tom Hume in the bottom of the seventh inning. Rafael Ramirez then hit a sacrifice fly to score Dale Murphy and close the lead to 3-2.

Bob Shirley relieved Tom Hume of a bases-loaded rally, striking out Chris Chambliss to end the eighth inning, with the Reds clinging to a 3-2 lead. The Braves were going into the ninth losing the game. In the 12 previous victories, the Braves always had the lead going into the ninth.

The Atlanta Braves offense threw the kitchen sink at the Reds in the ninth: A walk by leadoff batter Matt Sinatro, followed by a bunt for a base hit by Rafael Ramirez to bring in the runners on first and second. A flyball to centerfield for an out by Rufino Linares could not advance Sinatro to third. A slow rolling ball hit by Brett Butler to the shortstop struck the baserunner, Sinatro, in the spike causing Sinatro to be called out for interference, with Ramirez now at second, and Brett Butler at first, and it was two outs. But in a stroke of luck for the Braves, the ball that hit Sinatro stopped the play and a potential double-play opportunity by Dave Concepcion, a defensive whiz at shortstop who turned 1,290 double plays in his career for ninth-best among shortstops.

Jim Kern, a top reliever and a three-time All-Star came in to replace Bob Shirley, and then Joe Torre sent Biff Pocoroba to pinch hit for Glenn Hubbard. Kern uncorked a wild pitch, moving up Ramirez and Butler. Kern issued an intentional walk to Pocoroba to load the bases with two outs.

The Reds turned to tough lefty-throwing Joe Price to save the 3-2 lead against the Braves and Claudell Washington. Joe Price delivered a pitch that

Washington sent to center field scoring Ramirez and Butler for the walk-off win, taking the Braves to the incredible all-time record of 13 consecutive wins.

After the game, the question had to be asked if Matt Sinatro truly tried to evade the rolling ground ball, but Sinatro did not answer; instead, Joe Torre stepped in saying, "We do not train that kind of baseball."

The Braves' Bob Walk took the mound during the next game, and he pitched well attempting a 14th win. Bob Walk allowed two runs over 6 2/3 innings, but the Reds' Bruce Berenyi pitched just a little better with one run over 6 1/3 innings. Bruce Berenyi helped his own cause with an RBI single in the fifth in what turned out to be the decisive run in a 2-1 Reds victory.

There was no Matt Sinatro luck or wild pitches this ninth inning to push the Braves up as Glenn Hubbard hit a fly ball with Brett Butler on first, for the third out against Tom Hume, bringing the Braves record to an unbelievable 13-1.

Early on, Joe Torre was asked if he felt the Braves could back up Ted Turner's prediction that they could win the NL West. "I think we're capable, yes," Torre said in a 1982 Spring Training article in the *Sporting News*. "But whether you win it or not depends on so many things, including what the other teams in the division do. I haven't seen them all." The Braves now had a 3½ game lead over the Dodgers in the NL West and were making Ted Turner look like a genius.

For the 1982 Braves, 13 would have to be their lucky number. As of 2025, that record is still unbroken, but it was tied by the 1987 Milwaukee Brewers and the 2023 Tampa Bay Rays.

The Braves surprised with all the wins to start the season, but as quickly as they won the 13 games in a row, they gave a chunk right back by losing their next five games, all at home. They lost each game played April 21-27 against the Reds, Padres, and Pirates. The Braves had been up 4.5 games in the division just days before, but after losing 10-4 against the Pirates, the Braves choked away their lead in the standings and were left tied by April 28.

The Braves finally shook off their losing streak of five games, as they defeated the Pirates in a spectacular walk-off. The Braves starting pitcher that night was the ace of the staff and was looked to stop the bleeding. Phil Niekro responded well in the first two innings and appeared to be cruising to start the third, leading to a groundout by Dale Berra and striking out Eddie Solomon. Then trouble started as the speedy Omar Moreno doubled to right field. Then back-to-back walks to Johnny Ray and the Hall of Famer Dave Parker loaded the bases. The next four Pirates all singled, and the Braves were down 5–0 before Dale Berra came to bat for the second time in the inning flying out to end the inning. The Baseball-Reference win probability gave the Pirates a 92 percent chance of winning the game at that point. The Braves would have to fight back hard to win the game.

Phil Niekro came out for the fourth inning and promptly gave up a single to the pitcher, Eddie Solomon. The next batter was Omar Moreno, but the unlikely does happen in baseball. Moreno only grounded into one double play in all of 1981, and he had already done so earlier in the year. In fact, Moreno only grounded into 45 double plays across 5,481 plate appearances in his 12-year Major League Baseball career, or just once every 121.8 plate appearances.

Yes, you know where this is going.

Moreno hit a groundball to second baseman Glenn Hubbard who sent it to shortstop Rafael Ramirez, who then sent it back across the diamond to first baseman Chris Chambliss in time to get the speedy Moreno to complete the double play. Phil Niekro proceeded to strike out Johnny Ray to end the inning.

Phil Niekro pitched the fifth inning without giving up a run, and Joe Torre turned the ball to the bullpen starting in the sixth, with the Braves down 5–1 after an error eventually led to a Braves run in the bottom of the fourth inning.

Larry McWilliams shut the Pirates down in the sixth and seventh innings, and the Braves began to chip away at the Pirates lead in the bottom of the sixth. Glenn Hubbard played the "table setter" with a base hit to set up Claudell

Washington to hit a home run to center field to knock Eddie Solomon out and bring the game to 5–3.

The score remained a 5–3 Pirates lead going into the bottom of the eighth inning, with the Braves "meat of the order" coming up with their 2-3-4 batters.

After Hubbard flew out to start the inning, Washington belted a double to left field. Dale Murphy then took Paul Moskau deep for a 2-run home run and tied the game at 5. Bob Horner was the next batter and also took Moskau deep, this one to center field. The Braves were now up 6–5 and had erased their 5–0 deficit. Rod Scurry came into the game to complete the inning for Moskau, getting the second and third outs of the inning.

The ball was going to Gene Garber for the top of the ninth to shut the Pirates down for a Braves win. But speed kills. Omar Moreno led off with a single to right field. He then took off with the first pitch to the next batter and stole second base for his 10th stolen base in the young season. A ground ball moved Moreno to third base, putting Dave Parker to the plate with a runner in scoring position. Parker did his job and drove Moreno home with a single to tie the game at 6–6. As I wrote earlier, speed kills and it goes both ways. Dave Parker wanted to get into scoring position with the power hitting first baseman Jason Thompson coming up. Thompson was amid a 31-home-run, 32-double, 101-RBI season, and Parker wanted to give the Pirates a chance to take the lead with a hit out of the infield.

Dave Parker took off from first base with the first pitch from Garber to the cleanup hitter, Jason Thompson, but Parker was not fast enough as Benedict fired to Ramirez for the second out. Parker was not as proficient a base stealer as he had been earlier in his career, and for the season had only seven steals in 12 attempts. Thompson ended up striking out for the third out of the inning to set up the bottom of the ninth for the Braves to bat.

Rod Scurry, still pitching for the Pirates, sent the Braves down in order, and the game was now going into extra innings. Rick Camp replaced Gene Garber to pitch the 10th inning and set the Pirates "3 up and 3 down," handing the game to Braves' bats for the bottom of the 10th. And just like in life, sometimes in baseball it is better to be lucky than good, and the bottom of the tenth had a little of both.

Scurry took the mound for his third inning of relief. Claudell Washington hit a groundball to Scurry for the first out. Dale Murphy popped up for the second out. Bob Horner came up and worked a walk from Scurry. Chris Chambliss doubled to right field. Horner and Chambliss represented little to no speed at second and third bases, with two outs.

The Pirates brought in Kent Tekulve, a submariner who could easily induce a ground ball for the third out. The Braves had recently acquired from the Yankees, Bob Watson, coming to bat to pinch hit for Bruce Benedict. With the nickname of Bull, the now 36-year-old Watson was past his peak speed, but as a veteran hitter he was a good choice to win the game with a solid hit to the outfield.

It seemed like the Pirates manager Chuck Tanner had pulled the right string as the lumbering Watson hit a ground ball to Dale Berra at shortstop, but Berra misplayed the ball allowing Watson to get to first base and Bob Horner to score the winning run.

The Braves and Joe Torre went out for the game that night knowing they had to win for the chance to stay in first place. Although it was just April, they understood how to battle, and down five runs, they fought for the win and the right to stay in first place. The Braves were learning how to win and would remain in first place until the dog days of August. But it wasn't always easy.

With the challenge to the Brave's first place position stared down over the Pirates in a walk-off win fashion, the Braves then closed out April of 1982 with a pair of wins over the Cubs.

On April 29, Braves rookie pitcher Joe Cowley answered the bell against Hall of Fame Cubs pitcher Fergie Jenkins by going seven scoreless innings.

Jenkins retired Glenn Hubbard with a groundout for the first out in the bottom of the eighth, but trouble started for the Cubs when Claudell

Washington hit a single, stole second base, and took third on a throwing error by the catcher on the attempt to throw him out. Washington was on third with just one out; it was going to be an uphill battle for the Cubs with Dale Murphy and Bob Horner coming up.

The threat of a sacrifice fly was quickly dismissed as Dale Murphy struck a home run to left field to score Washington making it 2–0. For good measure, Bob Horner followed with his own shot to left field for a home run for a 3–0 lead. It was back-to-back home runs for Murphy and Horner again, after smashing back-to-back home runs just the night before against the Pirates. Murphy and Horner picked the bottom of the eighth again for their tandem power display. The Braves secured the shutout with the strong relief of Gene Garber getting credit for the win and Larry McWilliams and Rick Camp for the save.

On April 30, Steve Bedrosian spread four hits around seven innings against the Cubs, allowing no runs, and Gene Garber continued with two innings without a run for a 1–0 shutout. Claudell Washington provided all the offense needed by going 3–4 with a solo home run in the sixth inning.

It wasn't just Murphy and Horner winning games for the Braves in April 1982; Bob Watson was doing it too, but not necessarily on the field. The recently acquired Watson was a veteran with respect in the young locker room. That season he became a mentor to the young players offering batting guidance, acting as a sounding board, and providing a steady voice amplifying model behavior.

Claudell Washington was struggling much of that April, hitting just .188 with no home runs and 5 RBIs through April 27 before breaking out against the Cubs. An article in the *Sporting News* on May 24, 1982, shed some light on how this breakout may have happened. "He [Bob Watson] made the difference," explained Claudell Washington. "Bob told me I wasn't transferring my weight to my front-foot and therefore wasn't driving the ball. Balls I normally would drive into alleys, I was just hanging up in the air. I was hitting off my heels.

As soon as I followed his advice, I started driving the ball again," Washington concluded. After Watson's advice on April 27, Washington was 14–32 for a .438 batting average, with three home runs, and nine RBIs over the next seven games. Washington's batting average rose 105 points to .293 with the hot streak.

Even offensive stars like Dale Murphy and Bob Horner approached Bob Watson to discuss hitting. But Watson was careful not to offend or upset coaches and players with his mentorship.

"Joe Torre didn't ask me to do this, but he didn't say not to do it," Watson said. "I cleared it with the coaches anyway. The last thing I want to do is step on someone else's job. But I have the greenlight to express my opinions. And I'll be the first to tell you that I don't know it all," explained Watson on his leadership.

Bob Watson of course knew his hitting, and when he retired after the 1984 season, he became a hitting coach for the Oakland Athletics. Watson and Torre proved in 1982 that they could work well together, and that knowledge would serve them both well.

In no small part because of Bob Watson and Claudell Washington, the Braves were 16–5 at the end of April 1982 with a two-game lead in the NL over the San Diego Padres, with the Los Angeles Dodgers well behind at six games.

Joe Torre didn't seem to mind that Bob Watson was helping out the young players. "I guess it is unusual for a new guy to come in and feel comfortable so fast," Torre said. "But everybody here knows Watson's record as a hitter, and you naturally respect what he says. I like it because his ideas about hitting are sound. Actually, his basic premise is the same as mine—that a good hitter must hit to all fields," said Joe Torre in the same May 24, 1982, *Sporting News* article by Tim Tucker.

Many years later during an interview for this book, Joe Torre still remembers the thoughts he shared with Dale Murphy in 1982 about the batting that would work well for Murphy going forward and how to perhaps change his approach at the plate. Torre said, "I am not sure who the hitting coaches were that initially tried to make him pull the ball a lot because of his strength. But I felt that with our ballpark he could hit the ball out anywhere, right, center or left field"

Torre understood the best hitters had to keep working to use the whole field and that Murphy could do the same. "I thought he was a better hitter when he tried to hit the ball to whole field with his strength and power. We always had a good relationship as manager-player. We still have a good relationship today," explained Torre.

May of 1982 did not bring flowers for the Atlanta Braves as they went 11-15 for the month with just a paltry win streak of three games. The highlight of the month may have been a walk-off home run by Biff Pocoroba against the Saint Louis Cardinals on May 14. Phil Niekro pitched a sparkling eight innings of shutout ball handing the ball to Gene Garber for the ninth. The Pocoroba blast bailed Garber out from the loss after he allowed the game to be tied by a Keith Hernandez sacrifice fly in the top of the ninth inning for Garber's first blown save of the season.

The Braves lost seven of eight games to close out May but were miraculously up 1.5 games on the San Diego Padres with a 27-20 record. However, trouble was lurking as the World Series Champion Los Angeles Dodgers began to warm up with 15 wins for the month and closing the gap to four games behind the Braves. The Braves needed to get hot again for May to hold off the contenders in the NL West.

The Braves did just that by winning eight of their first nine games in June 1982, to bring their record up to 35-21 with a two-game lead in the NL West by June 12. The better news was that the Dodgers were slipping all the way to eight games behind. The Braves muddled to an 8-8 record as they were treading water going into back-to-back walk-off wins against the Astros to close out June.

The game on June 29, 1982, did not start out well for the Braves as Bob Walk served up a leadoff home run to left field from Dickie Thon. The Astros scored one in the first inning and brought the score of 5-0 into the bottom of the sixth inning as the Braves began to claw back into the game against a knuckleball sibling, Joe Niekro. A Brett Butler strikeout and a Glenn Hubbard groundout were two quick outs for the Braves, but consecutive singles by Claudell Washington, Dale Murphy, and Bob Horner scored one run, and a wild pitch to Chris Chambliss allowed a second run to score for the inning bringing the score to a more manageable 5–2 Astros advantage.

The Braves took a long way around to tie the game in the bottom of the seventh. The bottom of the order of 7-8-9 hitters did the job getting on base with consecutive singles and a walk to load the bases. Singles by Glenn Hubbard and Claudell Washington tied the game at 5–5 before Dale Murphy grounded out to end of the inning.

The score would remain knotted all the way to the bottom of the 11th inning as Rufino Linares, Brett Butler, and Glenn Hubbard each hit a single for the winning run. The Braves had big boppers like Murphy and Horner, but they won the game without power. All 12 hits were singles, and six other baserunners were from walks from the Astros. The Braves were learning to take what the opponents were giving them and win with it.

The June 30 game was a different script for the Braves. Phil Niekro pitched eight innings, only allowing two earned runs, but he found himself down 3–0 with a passed ball going into the bottom of the fourth. Bob Horner took Bob Knepper deep for his 12th home run of the year with a shot to left field in the fourth, making the score 3–1.

Joe Torre took the ball from Phil Niekro after the eighth inning, bringing in Carlos Diaz to pitch the top of the ninth with the Braves still down 3–1. A double by Jose Cruz, followed by a Ray Knight double brought the lead up to 4–1 for the Astros going into the bottom of the ninth.

Astros manager Bill Virdon decided to leave Bob Knepper in the game without going to the bullpen for a victory against the meat of the Braves lineup of 3-4-5. This turned out to be a poor managerial decision by Virdon. Dale Murphy led the inning with a home run to right field. Bob

Horner came up next and deposited a ball into the left field seats for his second home run of the game to bring the score to 4–3, putting the Astros' lead in jeopardy. Knepper still in the game gave up consecutive singles to Rufino Linares and Chris Chambliss before turning the ball over to Randy Moffitt with two men on base, and no outs. A force out at third base by Bruce Benedict and a walk to pinch hitter Larry Whisenton left it bases loaded with one out for another late-game heroics opportunity for the pinch-hitting Biff Pocoroba.

Pocoroba hit a single to right field to score Whisenton and Jerry Royster for the walk-off victory. Once again Pocoroba came through as Torre hit all the right managerial buttons by trusting his veteran pitcher to pitch eight full innings, his good bullpen use, and the right bats of the bench delivering in clutch situations.

So three walk-off wins made the Braves 18–9 for June, their most wins in a month during the season. The Braves were just .500 at home in June with a 6–6 record but shined on the road with a 12–3 record. The Braves lost one game each on the road to the Giants, Reds, and Astros.

On July 1 Braves fans looked at the Braves with their 45–29 record with a .608 winning percentage as the best in Major League Baseball with a three-game lead over the San Diego Padres and opening a six-game lead over the Los Angeles Dodgers.

✷✷✷

The front office for the 1982 Braves was led by John Mullen as the general manager. The Braves made some June moves that would end up paying off for the short term, but that didn't work out for them in the long term, and which ultimately proved to be a Braves valiant effort to get a young pitcher who would become one of the most dominating pitchers in baseball history.

On June 7 the Braves selected Zane Smith in the third round and Randy Johnson in the fourth round of the 1982 Amateur Draft, and on June 30, they traded Larry McWilliams to the Pittsburgh Pirates for a player to be named later and Pascual Perez. Minor leaguer infielder Carlos Rios came to the Braves on September 8 to complete the deal. The deal paid quick dividends for the Braves with Perez pitching in key spots down the stretch for the Braves. He spent the next seven years in AA-AAA for the Braves. Rios spent his entire career in the minor leagues appearing in 1,252 games without a major league appearance. Zane Smith climbed the ranks quickly making his major league debut for the Braves in 1984.

The sting from the Braves 1982 Major League Amateur Draft was that they were not able to sign Randy Johnson, a future Hall of Famer, with 303 wins, and one of the most dominating fastballs in Major League Baseball history. The Braves could not agree with the Californian 6'10" lefty from Livermore High School on a signing bonus. Johnson decided to stay on the West Coast and pitch college baseball at the University of Southern California for three seasons. Randy Johnson was later drafted in the second round and signed by the Montreal Expos in 1985. The Braves were not able to use a second-round pick in the 1985 MLB June Amateur Draft after forfeiting their pick for the 1984 signing of closing pitcher Bruce Sutter.

The Braves also drafted Urban Meyer in the 13th round in 1982. The future NCAA and NFL head coach did sign with the Braves, playing two seasons of rookie ball for the Braves as a shortstop, second baseman, third baseman, and catcher batting .182, with one home run, and driving in 11 runs.

★★★

The Braves were quick to capitalize on the two walk-off wins at the end of June by winning seven of eight games to start July, but quickly gave up their traction as they lost three of the last four games going into the All-Star break.

The Braves were not only the best in the National League with a 51–33 record and a .607 winning percentage, but they were also the best in all of Major League Baseball. But the San Diego Padres with their 50 wins were second and only two games back in the standings, and the Los Angeles Dodgers were still within eyesight at seven games back.

As good as the Braves' record was at the All-Star break, the 373 runs they scored versus the 324 runs they allowed, using the Pythagorean winning percentage of .564 shows that the Braves were winning more games than they "should" have won. The expected standings would have had the Padres ahead of the Braves with a .572 winning percentage through the first half of the season with the Braves at .564, and the Montreal Expos best in the NL East with .547, over the .527 of the Philadelphia Phillies. But as the saying goes, "that's why we play the games."

Is it better to be lucky than good, or maybe lucky and good, or even lucky and then good? Either way, the 1982 Braves were winning, and Joe Torre was making the right calls to give his team a chance to win the NL West. Torre was making a strong case for a Wins Above Replacement (WAR) number for a manager.

The Braves team took the break, and Dale Murphy, Bob Horner, and Phil Niekro were selected for the All-Star game played in Montreal.

The Atlanta Braves would need to keep winning.

The Braves came out of the All-Star break hitting on all cylinders on the road as they rolled over the Chicago Cubs winning 3 of 4 games, outscoring the Cubs 27–14, with the only loss being a walk-off win by the Cubs from a Jay Johnstone hit off Gene Garber during the bottom of the 10th on July 16.

The Braves continued their road trip by taking two of three games in Saint Louis against the Cardinals. In a game that baseball purists would be sure to love, Phil Niekro, against the Cardinals Ace, Joaquín Andujar, pitched 7 1/3 innings, allowing one run, bringing his record to 8–3, and Gene Garber came in for 1 2/3 innings of relief and his 18th save. The game was played in exactly two hours.

Much like Joe Torre believed in hitting to all fields during at-bats to give players their best chance for success, a strong case could be made that the 1982 Braves could adjust their offense for a different kind of playing surface. Grass versus artificial turf (or Astroturf as it was called back in the day), was played on for approximately 40 percent of games during 1970–1990.

Atlanta-Fulton County Stadium was not artificial turf, but the Braves would have to play on it when on the road, and their offense looked different when they did. Baseball played differently on concrete over lime-green carpet. The ball played faster on the ground, hops were higher, a ball driven into the ground with a high hop could take a funny bounce or make it easier for a speedy runner to get on base.

Players like Omar Moreno, Tim Raines, Willie McGee, Lonnie Smith, Vince Coleman, and Willie Wilson with blazing speed could become a star without having a big power bat. Players with good power could find the gaps into the alley, players like George Brett, Frank White, and Willie Aikens.

A hard-batted ball that finds the outfield turf could roll fast and forever, resulting in easy doubles and triples. Players from artificial turf teams led the National League, such as Al Oliver of the Expos with 43 doubles and Dickie Thon of the Astros with 10 triples. Hal McRae of the Royals led Major League Baseball in doubles with 46 and triples with 15. His doubles-machine teammate, Frank White, hit 45.

Teams had to adapt to the turf, and Joe Torre and the Braves understood that, so two Braves teams developed. Dale Murphy saw players like Brett Butler change how the Braves were going to play on the road while on artificial turf. "Brett came up in 1982 and gave us some spark that we needed. Brett had speed, some power, stole bases for us. Our team wasn't really known for stealing bases and things like that, but he gave us a more well-rounded attack. Claudell Washington, and Brett set that up for us," said Murphy.

But the power was not as effective away from home, or on artificial turf. "We had power, me, Chambliss, and Bob Horner, and our bench as well. We were able to set the tone for that club, with Fulton County Stadium, we were going to have an advantage with our power, and now with the speed we had, it played into all the ballparks that had the turf," explained Dale Murphy.

So there was the home-field team–the "Sultan of Swat" home-run-hitting team in Atlanta driving up TBS ratings–and the team on the road, which was not hitting home runs. The Braves led the National League in 1982 with 146 home runs. The second highest was the Los Angeles Dodgers with 138. The two teams that were lowest in home runs were the turf teams of the Astros at 74, and the Saint Louis Cardinals at 67. Now with a Jekyll and Hyde approach, the Braves were going to adapt to win games on artificial turf, and on the road. The 1982 Braves were a blistering .580 on the road versus a .519 at home.

Of the 146 Braves home runs in 1982, 126 were at grass fields with just 20 on the road. The Braves were able to drive the ball out of the park once every 36.52 plate appearances or once every 32.58 at-bat. Artificial turf showed a completely different approach, resulting in one for 81.55 plate appearances or 71.95 at-bats. Power hitters like Dale Murphy played a different offensive game on artificial turf and it showed.

Murphy hit 32 of 36 home runs on grass at one per 16 plate appearances, or one per 14 at-bats. He did not display the over the fence hitting with four home runs on artificial turf, one per 37.25 at-bats, or 46 plate appearances. Murphy seemed to have better plate discipline by averaging a walk for 8.7 plate appearance against a lower rate of 5.4 on grass.

Even on the bases it was different for Murphy. On grass, he attempted to steal a base once every 15 times on base, whereas on artificial turf, he attempted a more conservative once every 23 times on base. Overall, he seemed to be a less impactful hitter evidenced by an outstanding Ops+ of 167 on grass, and a below-league average of 90 on artificial turf.

Bob Horner hit a total of 32 home runs, just five of them on artificial turf fields. He hit a home run for every 15.3 plate appearances, or 13.25 at-bats on grass versus one per 31.6 plate appearances, or 28.2 at-bats on artificial turf. Joe Torre must have felt the slow-footed Horner could steal a base or two. Horner attempted to steal a base just once per 138 plate appearances on grass versus once per 31.6 on artificial turf. He had a higher Ops+ of 144 on artificial turf versus 135 on grass.

The 1982 "Turf Team" did not do as well as they wanted by winning two of three against the Saint Louis Cardinals, and then losing two of three to the Pittsburgh Pirates on the artificial turf fields. The Braves were outscored a combined 32–16, shutout in back-to-back games and in three of the six games played.

The home-run-dependent Braves were only able to stroke out one home run (Glenn Hubbard) over the six games, while the competition slugged four of them. The Braves tried to generate runs and make things happen on the basepaths, but with mixed results of five stolen bases in 11 tries, with two unlikely Braves (Chris Chambliss and Bob Horner) stealing bases. The Pirates and Cardinals had accomplished base stealers like Omar Moreno, Lonnie Smith, and Tommy Herr, and those teams did better with six stolen bases in nine attempts.

Joe Torre allowed his players to be aggressive on the bases. Speed is only part of being a successful baserunner; there are also baseball instincts like anticipation, reading the ball, knowing the baseball situation to be aggressive, and trusting your teammates. The Braves displayed all of this.

The 1982 Braves, with their 18 swipes of third base, were second only to the Padres who had 19. Going first to third is another example of a good running team, and the Braves were tied with the Padres for having a runner from first base reach third base, or score when a single is hit. The Braves were second in the National League to the Cardinals with a runner from second base scoring on a single. The Braves were also good at moving runners over into scoring position. Their 96 sacrifice bunts were only second to the Dodgers who had 106.

The composite of the offense showed that the Braves were a very young team, with an average age of 27 with the 39 batters that year, the second youngest offense to the Padres at 26.6 years old. The Braves displayed the patience to sacrifice runners, being aggressive on the basepaths and putting runners into scoring position, and they had the strength and maturity to lead the National League in home runs.

The "Turf" model for the Braves may have been better in terms of winning for the Braves as opposed to playing at home on their natural grass. The 1982 Braves were 42–39 at home with a .519 win-loss percentage, but were 47–34 with a .580 percentage on the road, specifically with a 23–16 on away grass fields, but also able to not be small-balled, or run out of the artificial turf games, by going 24–18 and winning .571 percent of their games on artificial turf. The Braves combine for 65 of their 89 wins on grass for a .541 winning percentage, as compared to a 30 percent higher winning percentage on artificial turf. The Braves were a team winning at home, away, on grass, and on artificial turf; it didn't matter.

The Braves were back at home in late July to face the National League West second place San Diego Padres for four games. The Braves had a five-game lead in the standing over the Padres, but they had the chance to put the Padres in their rearview mirror by pulling off the sweep, or the Braves could allow the Padres to inch closer to them over the four games.

The Braves found their home run stroke that had been evading them against the Cardinals and Pirates the week before. They had lost to the Cardinals and Pirates by a combined score of 32–16, and only hitting one home run. The Braves broke out and flipped the script at home against the Padres by slugging

10 home runs over four games and sweeping the Padres by a combined score of 32–16.

Dale Murphy slugged three home runs over the four games, and Bob Horner knocked two out as well. The Braves did not steal a base, with Claudell Washington being thrown out in the sole attempt to steal a base, but during the four-game series, the Padres and Braves went a combined two stolen bases in four attempts. During the last five games on turf that the Braves had played, the Braves, Cardinals, and Pirates went combined for 11 stolen bases in 20 attempts. It was indeed a different kind of baseball, and the Braves found ways to dominate and be versatile.

It was all falling into place for the Braves, and for two of their best players it was especially sweet after years of looking up into the standings. It was a better view from atop the NL West, and they were enjoying the view their two young stars were finally hitting their stride as the Braves were loving life at the top of Major League Baseball.

Dale Murphy

For once, Dale Murphy was on top looking down, but as we reflect, we can see Murphy, arguably, as the best baseball player of the 1980s.

Many fans admire Dale Murphy not just because of what he did on the baseball field, but also for the kind of person he was, his courage to take a strong stance on performance-enhancing drugs, and his personal views on conduct and religion.

Joe Torre, a man of incredible character and decades of being in baseball locker rooms knows a thing or two about great players and about people. "As a manager, you want him [Murphy] as a player. If you're a father, you want him as a son. If you're a woman, you want him as a husband. If you're a kid, you want him as a father. What else can you say about him?" said Joe Torre.

Dale Murphy was a 6'4" 210-pound hitting machine playing Gold Glove defense, hitting bombs, and saying *and* doing the right things off the field as well.

Baseball has had its share of heroes and villains, but it seems like the players who blend dominance with controversy are beloved and remembered more. Hank Aaron, a less flashy player, is often grouped with fellow outfielders like Mickey Mantle and Willie Mays. Babe Ruth as amazing a player as he was, is almost certainly seen now as a cartoon character of excess; a large, fat player who drank way too much, womanized, and created headlines with a load of boastful claims.

Dale Murphy and his humble, clean-living lifestyle are not much of an exaggeration or manufactured media clips. Rather, his habits off the diamond are simply a part of who he is. A member of the Church of Jesus Christ of Latter-day Saints, Murphy does not drink alcoholic beverages, would not allow photos of women embracing him, and would often pay his teammates' dinner checks if alcoholic beverages were not on the tab.

Murphy would refuse to give television interviews unless he was fully dressed, and he was not in favor of female reporters in the locker room. Murphy would even do endorsements for milk and ice cream.

Murphy's propensity to do good things almost made him bite off more than he could chew on June 12, 1983. He was visiting with Elizabeth Smith, a six-year-old girl who lost both hands and a leg after stepping on a live power line. During the conversation with the child and her nurse, Murphy somehow agreed to hit her a home run that night. True to form, Dale Murphy overdelivered by hitting two home runs driving in all three runs in a 3–2 victory.

"Just look at him over there. Doesn't drink, doesn't smoke, doesn't take greenies, nicest guy you'd ever want to meet, hits the hell out of the ball, hustles like crazy, plays a great centerfield and isn't trying to get anything from anybody.... Doesn't he just make you sick?" said Terry Forster, a former teammate in *Sports Illustrated* during 1985.

But when looking at Dale Murphy solely from within the context of the 1980s, it is hard to argue that he was perhaps the most dominant player. During the 1980s Dale Murphy did the following:

- Hit 308 home runs to finish just behind Mike Schmidt's 313 home runs.
- Drove home 929 RBI tying Mike Schmidt for the NL lead, and second in MLB to Eddie Murray.
- Paced the NL with 938 runs, good for fourth in MLB.

In 2019, ESPN did a piece compiling a 1980s MLB All-Decade Team. In the article by David Schoenfield, he selected the following players:

- C Gary Carter: 118 OPS+, 44.9 WAR
- 1B Eddie Murray: 141 OPS+, 45.9 WAR
- 2B Ryne Sandberg: 112 OPS+, 37.7 WAR
- 3B Mike Schmidt: 153 OPS+, 56.6 WAR
- SS Cal Ripken: 123 OPS+, 50.2 WAR
- OF Rickey Henderson: 137 OPS+, 71.1 WAR
- OF Robin Yount: 135 OPS+, 55.3 WAR
- OF Dale Murphy: 132 OPS+, 47.1 WAR
- DH Wade Boggs: 150 OPS+, 60.2 WAR

The most obvious point is that every player on the list except Dale Murphy is in the Hall of Fame. Six of the nine players walked into the Hall of Fame during their first year of eligibility. Gary Carter had to sweat through six years of voting, and Ryne Sandberg had to wait three. Not even Cy Young, Joe DiMaggio, Yogi Berra, or Eddie Mathews walked in during their first year of eligibility.

There was outrage when Ichiro Suzuki did not become the second player to be unanimously voted into Cooperstown; Mariano Rivera was the first. Dale Murphy was a more dominant player than Suzuki, so if folks were so upset about Suzuki, why not also about Murphy? Perhaps most in arms about the one vote short for Suzuki was *Boston Globe* columnist Bob Ryan writing that the lone holdout "should have his or her voting rights revoked and should be placed under House Arrest because clearly that person is unhinged and a clear danger to Society."

Ichiro Suzuki was a little more lighthearted as shown during a press conference held shortly after his election to the Hall of Fame in January of 2025. "I've been coming to the Hall of Fame as a player seven times, and this is my eighth time here in the Hall of Fame, and what an honor it is for me to be here as a Hall of Famer," Ichiro said through an interpreter. "This is a very special moment. I was able to receive many votes from the writers, and [I'm] grateful for them, but there's one writer that I wasn't able to get a vote from. I would like to invite him over to my house, and we'll have a drink together, and we'll have a good chat."

Ichiro was named on 393 of 394 ballots, and it is considered a travesty of a vote. Perhaps Dale Murphy should invite some voters himself over a tall glass of cold milk to discuss why he is still waiting. But Murphy would need to have a lot of milk to pour.

Dale Murphy has been on the Hall of Fame ballot 15 times; 1982 was the year with his most votes—116 out of 499—which was only 23.2% of the ballots cast. Instead of a steady rise during the years that followed, he dipped to as low as 8.5%. Those 43 votes were just a stone's throw from the minimum 5 percent needed to avoid being booted for failing to achieve the minimum needed to stay on the ballot.

The Dale Murphy Hall of Fame candidacy was reconsidered with the Classic Baseball Committee in 2018, and at a Contemporary Baseball Committee 2022 voting, he did not receive a single vote. Murphy did better during his 2022 Contemporary Baseball Era vote accruing 6 of 16 votes, but still well below the 12 needed for induction.

Nobody ever said that the Baseball Hall of Fame—or its election process—are perfect; the voters try. But it seems like there are still exhausting narratives, personal thinking, and group thinking in the results. Let's look at the results for "Player A" and "Player B," in the box, below.

Player "A"	Player "B"
398 home runs	117 home runs
1,266 RBIs	780 RBIs
265 BA	311 BA
346 OBP	355 OBP
469 SLG	402 SLG
815 OPS	757 OPS
OPS+ 121	107 OPS+
WPA 30.4	

Baseball Analytics has shifted attention away from the traditional back-of-the-baseball-card numbers. The triple crown numbers of batting average (BA), home runs (HRs), and runs batted in (RBIs) used to be the standard to gauge the best MLB batters. The baseball media, voters, now consider advanced analytics like on-base percentage (OBP), on-base plus slugging (OPS), and on-base plus slugging plus (OPS+) to delineate the best players as superior to singles and batting average.

This is why it is surprising that "Player A" is Dale Murphy and "Player B" is Ichiro Suzuki, with one drawing a standing ovation for Cooperstown, and the other receiving the cold shoulder.

Murphy seems to understand that perhaps he was not able to compile some of the milestone numbers of 400 or 500 home runs, or 3,000 hits, due to injuries slowing him down as his career went on. "It seems my career fell just short, I was simply not able to stay healthy long enough and get to the numbers the voters wanted I guess," explained Dale Murphy on falling short of Cooperstown so far.

Bob Horner

If Dale Murphy was Captain America for the Braves in the 1980s, Bob Horner could be seen as a cartoon character resembling Yosemite Sam, but that image would be superficial, without giving Horner the courtesy of a deeper look.

Bob Horner seemed like everything Dale Murphy was not. At 6'1" and 195 pounds, Horner seemed shorter, heavier, and wider on the ball field, with a magnificent blond mullet flowing from his ball cap. It would have been easy to imagine Horner rolling up to a recreational softball team, just one of the guys playing the afternoon away. But that would grossly underestimate him and his competitive team-first personality.

Bob Horner went to the Braves in 1978, direct from their MLB draft as the first player taken overall. His 23 home runs in 323 at-bats quickly validated the Atlanta Braves bold choice to have him skip Minor League Baseball entirely.

Horner played through many injuries but was still not able to compile more than 140 games in a single season. He was able to put up big seasons with Dale Murphy allowing the duo to become one of the most powerful tandems in MLB history.

As the 1978 Rookie of the Year, Horner produced solid power numbers, which afforded Murphy protection in the lineup, and in turn, Horner was protected by Murphy, the two of them switching back-and-forth around the steady veteran power bat of Chris Chambliss. Murphy could not be pitched around, which allowed him to become a solid player bordering on All-Star and he became a true superstar of the game.

Dale Murphy had to adapt over the course of his major league career, especially with his position in the field. He had been drafted as a catcher in 1974, and he made his debut as a catcher in 1976. Murphy played 37 games 1976–1977, starting all his games as a catcher. But he developed a throwing issue with his return throws to the mound or on attempted steals going wild and allowed an alarming 14 passed balls behind the plate. Base runners had a license to steal against Murphy with just a 23 percent caught stealing rate.

Going into 1978, the Braves had a problem behind the plate defensively with their two young catchers. The 22-year-old Dale Murphy had not flashed the defensive skills to stay behind the plate, and the 24-year-old Biff Pocoraba had the second most passed balls in the National League in 1977 at 15.

Dale Murphy with his power potential was moved to first base, and Biff Pocoraba set up behind the dish. "Give Murphy 500 at-bats this season, and he'll hit 25 homers minimum in the National League," said Bobby Cox.

Cox's first year as the Braves manager was 1978, and his moves looked both good and then bad by the end of the season. Dale Murphy came close to the predicted 25 home runs in 500 at-bats by hitting 23 home runs in 530 at-bats. Biff Pocoraba was the primary catcher and made the NL All-Star team.

But the bad reared its ugly head with Dale Murphy leading NL first basemen (and all NL batters) with 20 errors; the second most errors were made by Tony Perez of the Montreal Expos with 11. Murphy also paced the National League with 145 strikeouts. Biff Pocoraba was again second in the league in passed balls and only threw out 23.4 percent of steal attempts.

But there was good news again! Catcher Bruce Benedict made his MLB debut on August 18, 1978, his 23rd birthday, and got a base hit in his first at-bat. Benedict played in 22 games down the stretch for the Braves, not allowing a passed ball and threw out 40.7 percent of would-be stealers. Benedict would remain a mainstay as the Braves catcher all the way through 1989; he is fourth in innings on the Braves All-Time innings played as a catcher.

The Braves' catching situation for 1979 had Joe Nolan and Bruce Benedict sharing the catching duties, with Dale Murphy only appearing in 27 games at catcher. An injured Biff Pocoroba forced Murphy to be the Opening Day catcher for 1979 and to start most of the first 30 games. Murphy caught the last game for his career on May 21, moving to first base with Bruce Benedict stepping in as the starting catcher.

Dale Murphy battled a knee injury throughout much of the 1979 season, even missing part of the season due to knee surgery. He appeared in 76 games at first base and 27 at catcher, and still managed to finish the season with 21 home runs and decreasing his errors to 15 from 20 at first base.

When you look at his 1979 season on defense, Dale Murphy was a disaster. He started 75 games as a first baseman with his 15 errors the second-highest in the league behind Cesar Cedeno of the Houston Astros, who had 17 errors. But as a double-whammy, Murphy was also second in the National League in passed balls in his 27 games behind the plate (10 games as Phil Niekro's catcher). The Atlanta Braves now placed second in passed balls for the three consecutive years of 1977–1979.

I do not want to place all the blame on the Braves catchers, however, for the three years of passed balls. As is often attributed to Bob Uecker, a former Major League Baseball catcher and play-by-play announcer, "The way to catch a knuckleball is to wait until it stops rolling and then pick it up." This quote was often made in reference to Uecker's time catching knuckleballer pitcher Phil Niekro while with the Braves. Phil Niekro may have had his three most prolific seasons 1977–1979 as he pitched 1,006.2 innings and led the National League each of those years in innings pitched and games started.

Bruce Benedict was behind the plate for 29 games catching Niekro, and still only allowed eight passed balls throughout the season catching all the Braves pitchers.

As bad as Murphy was on defense as a catcher and first baseman, his bat began to scream that he needed to be in the lineup. The knee injury saw his at-bats go from 530 in 1978 to 384 at-bats in 1979, but his numbers showed remarkable improvement if you look through his 21 home runs and 57 RBIs. His batting average went from .226 to .276, an increase of 50 points. His on-base percentage jumped from .284 to .340, and most startling was that his OPS+ (on-base plus slugging plus) rose dramatically from being a below-average MLB hitter of 80 in 1978 to 113 in 1979. The use of OPS+ is an effective tool for comparing players of the time and stands up well for comparing players across the years.

OPS+ takes a player's on-base plus slugging percentage and normalizes the number across the entire league. It accounts for external factors like ballparks. It then adjusts so a score of 100 is league average, and 150 is 50 percent better than the league average.

During the first half of Dale Murphy's 1979 season, as he was battling knee problems, his bat was red-hot. He looked like Johnny Bench offensively for those 27 games as a catcher through May 21, when Murphy had 11 home runs, 24 RBIs, and was batting .351.

With his knee barking and bat blazing, the Braves moved Murphy to first base for the rest of May, but then he was out for June and half of July as he opted for arthroscopic knee surgery.

Murphy was able to make it back into the lineup to finish the year, but his numbers were only 8 home runs, 21 RBIs, and .231 batting average. His Split OPS+ for the first half of the season was 194, with a Split OPS+ a 78 after his return. Of course, major league teams did not know OPS+ in 1979, but Murphy's Split OPS+ of 229 as a catcher through May 21 was much better than his Split OPS+ of 73 as a first baseman that year.

Was the much-improved bat of 1979 going to return after his knee fully recovered? Was there a spot for his bat in the lineup in 1980 with his defense such a liability? Could the team afford to keep Dale Murphy at first base, and if not him, then who, and where could he play otherwise?

The Braves answered that question in 1980 as they traded for former Gold Glover Chris Chambliss to play first base, moving Murphy to center field, and keeping former MVP Jeff Burroughs and 1979 All-Star Gary Matthews in the outfield. With no designated hitter at the time in the National League, this was going to be Dale Murphy's last chance for the Atlanta Braves. He was going to have to make it work, or he would be out of baseball, or he would have to switch to the American League as a designated hitter or pinch hitter.

The move worked for Dale Murphy as he proved healthy from his knee injury playing in 156 games, his bat returning to 1979 pre-injury form with 33 home runs and 89 RBIs, and making his first All-Star team while placing 12th in the 1979 MVP voting.

Perhaps just as importantly, Murphy showed he could hold his own in center field for the Braves. He had a solid .985 fielding percentage as center fielder, which was fifth in the National League; his 374 putouts as an outfielder was good for fifth in the National League, and his 11 assists from center field were good for third in the league. Murphy and the Braves were now in sync, and Murphy played the outfield for the rest of his career with the Braves.

But does Dale Murphy think he could have stayed behind the dish? "I had good potential at catcher. It just didn't work out that way. My defense wasn't that good; it didn't materialize into being the next Johnny Bench. There was some potential there, but you know, it worked out for me moving from catcher," explained Murphy.

Joe Torre knows how hard it is for a catcher to have to move positions. Torre himself was an All-Star catcher, but starting with his 1971 season through the end of his playing career, he manned the corners of the infield as a third baseman, and first baseman.

This move in 1971 from behind the dish to third base unleashed an MVP season for Torre, hitting .363, bringing home 137 runners, and knocking 230 hits all good for tops in the National League. At third base for the St. Louis Cardinals, Torre was able to stay healthy and play 161 games.

Joe Torre remembers how he would occasionally tease Murphy about moving positions again. "Every once in a while, I would tell Murph, he was going to have to play first base tomorrow, he would just say 'no-no-no' back while shaking his head," said Torre. "He always knew I was kidding; I never would have done anything from keeping him comfortable out there in the field."

And looking back, Torre still realizes what a treat it was to have a superstar player like Dale Murphy on his team. "We played him in center field, but I always thought, perhaps he was more comfortable in right field, but he was a gamer out there every day in center field. Everybody should have a chance managing a guy like Dale Murphy," reflected Torre on Murphy's team-first mentality.

5
Roller Coaster Going Down

On July 29, 1982, the Braves were the best they would be for the rest of the year. The four-game sweep of the Padres opened the lead in the National League West to what would be the highwater mark of nine games, and 24 games over .500 percent.

The Braves were now 61–37, with a .622 winning percentage. Nine games up on the Padres, 10 1/2 games up on the Dodgers, and easily leading the Phillies and the Saint Louis Cardinals by five games as the best record in the National League. No other MLB team was close to matching the Braves, with the Red Sox lagging behind with 58 wins, and a .586 winning percentage. But trouble was approaching the Atlanta Braves, in what some fans called the "Curse of Chief-Noc-A-Homa," and the Los Angeles Dodgers were coming to town.

The concept of a Braves mascot began in 1964, when Tim Rynders, a high school student, set up a tepee in the outfield of Milwaukee County Stadium, dressing as a Native American, dancing, and setting off smoke bombs with each Milwaukee Braves run. Rynders did not have a name for his character, nor was this officially a team mascot, but this became a beloved tradition for the fans.

Once the team moved to Atlanta, the Braves held a contest to name a mascot, and the character of Chief Noc-A-Homa was created. Larry Hunn, a local college student, was the first Chief Noc-A-Homa, before Tim Minors received the job. The first people to take on the role of Chief Noc-A-Homa were not Native Americans; but Levi Walker, a member of the Odawa tribe, believed the Chief should be played by a Native American, and he asked the Atlanta Braves to let him take over the character.

Levi Walker performed as the Chief from 1969 to 1986, in a 250-seat left field section, with his tepee sending smoke signals with each Braves home run and celebrating each run scored by the Braves. The Chief would also perform on the field during pregame festivities including a ceremony on the pitcher's mound.

Like many stadiums at the time, Atlanta-Fulton County Stadium was a multisport venue shared with the Atlanta Falcons of the National Football League. During every preseason, the seating arrangements would have to be modified for either baseball or football.

With the first-place Braves becoming must-see baseball across cable TV, and in-person in the stadium, team owner Ted Turner evicted the tepee in favor of additional seating for what seemed like a magical summer of winning and the hope of hitting the two-million mark in home attendance at Atlanta-Fulton County Stadium to see the Braves. The two million number had not been eclipsed in Atlanta and was last seen during the 1954–1957 seasons by the Milwaukee Braves. The Braves only hit the one million fan attendance once in the previous 10 years, in 1980 with 1,048,411 fans in the stadium.

With the World Champion Dodgers coming into town, Ted Turner made the decision to reconfigure the stadium seating to add 250 seats to the baseball capacity—thus matching the usual football-capacity seating—but taking over the area used by the Chief.

The Braves were about to duel with the Dodgers over four games, but for Ted Turner it may have felt more like a potential coronation, or an upcoming acknowledgment from the World Champion Dodgers that the Braves were going to be the next team to beat the American League in the World Series. A packed crowd of 47,787 fans, including former President Jimmy Carter, were there to see the greatness that had been the 1982 Braves up until then.

Ted Turner and Jimmy Carter were behind the Braves dugout, watching what looked like a runaway Braves victory as the team jumped to an 8–3 lead after five innings. Many teams playing on the road would have wilted under the pressure, but the Dodgers were not that team.

The two first Dodgers batters in the sixth were Co-MVPs of the 1981 World Series and were about to start a comeback. Pedro Guerrero led off with a single, and Ron Cey hit a home run to make it 8–5. The Braves countered by bringing in the recently unstoppable Steve Bedrosian as pitcher to induce a groundout from Steve Garvey and then striking out Mike Scioscia and Rick Monday.

The scoreless inning for Bedrosian brought his streak of scoreless innings to 28, and an incredible 31 of 34 batters. But then the wheels fell off the wagon during the next inning as Bedrosian was roughed up for five runs, putting the Dodgers up 10–8. The Braves tried to mount a comeback during the bottom of the ninth with three base hits, but they could only bring one run across, stranding two baserunners, and the Dodgers delivered a crushing loss at home in front of the packed house.

The typically media-friendly Braves manager, Joe Torre, was not as affable when he locked reporters out of the postgame clubhouse between the first and second games on July 30.

Even with Torre shielding his team from the media between the two games, the Braves came out flat for the second game that night, quickly falling behind 6–0. The Braves had little fight as the Dodgers Bob Welch pitched a complete game, scattering six hits and winning his 11th game of the year. The Murphy-Horner duo could not cause any damage going 0–7, striking out three times in eight plate appearances.

Joe Torre tried to downplay the losses to the Dodgers. "If we're nine games ahead and lose, and feel bad about it, there's something wrong," said Torre after the second game of the night.

In the third game, the Dodgers and Fernando Valenzuela disappointed a nearly sold-out stadium of 46,694 fans. Joe Torre tinkered with the lineup by moving Claudell Washington to leadoff and moving Murphy and Horner to third and fourth spots in the lineup. The changes did not work as Washington went 0-4, and Murphy and Horner were each able to just hit a single. Valenzuela dominated the Braves by pitching a complete game shutout for his 14th win of the year.

Bob Horner was dismissive of the doom and gloom the media was casting over the Braves after the loss. "Everybody's making too big a deal about this," said Horner. "We sweep the Padres, and they were writing off the other teams. We lose three, and they're trying to write us off. They have to go a ways to get us."

The Braves were looking to avoid a painful series sweep at home versus the Dodgers on Sunday afternoon of August 1. They had their pitching ace Phil Niekro on the mound, and the veteran Chris Chambliss quickly put the Braves out in front hitting a grand slam in the first inning for a 4-0 lead. Niekro uncharacteristically could only pitch four innings, giving up 10 base hits and 4 runs, before going to the bullpen. The Braves pitching could not shut the door against the Dodgers as Carlos Diaz and Gene Garber were battered for five more runs, while the Dodgers bullpen held the game in check for the eventual 9-4 Dodgers win and the four-game sweep in Atlanta.

The Braves had wanted to sink the Dodgers, but, instead, they gave life to the them. Dale Murphy and Bob Horner—as two of the best players in the National League—combined for three hits in 30 at-bats, all for singles, so it was going to be the dog days of August for the Braves. August started out badly and had the possibility of reaching a low of historic proportions before the month ended. Murphy had a realistic attitude after the four-game sweep by the Dodgers, "I don't think we can find a silver lining in this," said Murphy. "We've got to come back and create one. There's still a lot of baseball left."

The Braves had to stop the bleeding against the Giants, opening a three-game series on August 2, before having to start another west coast swing.

Bob Walk pitched well enough for the Braves to win his tenth game of the year by pitching seven innings, allowing eight hits and three runs. Steve

Bedrosian returned to form by pitching two scoreless frames for his seventh save and reducing his ERA to a sparkling 1.89. Bob Horner's bat sprung back to life going 2-4 with a homerun and two RBIs. Dale Murphy was still in a slump going 0-4.

The Braves were back in the win column with a 7-3 win. The Padres lost to the Astros 6-4, and the Dodgers were trounced on the road 5-1 in Cincinnati bringing the Braves seven games up on the Padres and 7 1/2 games up on the Dodgers. The Braves still had the best record in baseball after the August 2 game, and maybe the recent Dodgers sweep had been just a blip.

The Braves hopped out to a 3-0 lead during the next game against the Giants in the bottom of the third with a wild pitch scoring a run, and Bob Horner stayed hot with his second home run in two games, making the score 3-0. But the Braves would be stifled during the remainder of the game, eventually allowing four runs by the Giants in the ninth inning for a 6-3 loss. Dale Murphy was still looking for base hits and finished 0-4.

The Braves were looking to win another game in the three-game series to win at least two out of three games, to end their homestand on a high note. The top of the fourth inning saw a solo home run by the Giants Reggie Smith, and a single by Tom O'Malley off Joe Cowley to drive in Jeff Leonard for a 2-0 Giants lead. But the Braves were able to answer the bell during the bottom of the fourth inning.

Dale Murphy broke a skid by getting a single, and Bob Horner hit his third home run against the Giants over the three games for a 2-0 lead; that was Horner's 23rd home run of the year. Both teams went scoreless for the next four innings before the Giants broke the tie in the top of the ninth. After pitching a scoreless eighth inning, Steve Bedrosian stayed in the game for the ninth; this move to stick with Bedrosian looked solid as he retired Tom O'Malley with a fly ball and Darrell Evans struck out. But with two outs, the Giants scored on a single, stolen base, and on another single to make it a 3-2 lead going into the bottom of the ninth. The Braves did not have a comeback in them as Giants reliever Greg Milton came in to retire the Braves in order for a 3–2 Giants victory.

The good news was that Murphy and Horner started to hit again, with the heart of the Braves offense going 2–4. After the high point of July 29, and the removal of Chief Noc-A-Homa, the Braves were 1–6 and outscored by 42–27, and the Dodgers (after winning two of the three games against the Reds) were now just 4 1/2 games behind the Braves and in second place ahead of the Padres.

The Dodgers, after sweeping the Braves in Atlanta, were going to try to do the same in Los Angeles. If the Braves kept stumbling, they could lose a huge lead in the National League West standings, and for a young baseball team like the Braves it would not be unusual to falter in August. The Braves fought hard in Los Angeles over the next four games, usually in the lead, but still, somehow, they lost all four of the games in heartbreaking fashion.

For the Braves to be successful in the second half of the year they would need solid starting pitching, but coming out of the gate after the All-Star break, it was anything but solid. The Braves' starting pitching had a combined 5.12 ERA over the first 15 games post–All-Star break. Phil Niekro was still delivering for the Braves, and Rick Camp was still dependable, but Rick Mahler was dropped to the bullpen after having been the Braves' best starter earlier in the season.

"Our starting pitchers have to be more consistent," said Joe Torre at the time. "My assumption is that, for us to win the pennant, our starters are going to have to get us into the seventh inning regularly." The importance of getting that far into the game was to hand the ball over to an emerging Steve Bedrosian and an elite stopper in Gene Garber. Joe Torre mastered the technique of handing the ball off to an elite bullpen combination early on in his years with the New York Yankees with Mariano Rivera and John Wetteland for the 1996 Yankees.

Joe Torre was now going with Phil Niekro, Rick Camp, and Bob Walk up top, with rookies Joe Cowley and Pascual Perez rounding out the five-man rotation. Bob Walk was only 24 years old at the time, but he had already lived through a pennant chase and started a World Series game for the Championship 1980 Phillies and recognized the need of consistency from himself. "I can only speak for myself, and I know I need to be more consistent... not have a good outing, bad outing, good outing, bad, good, bad," Walk explained at the time.

The Saint Louis Cardinals were watching the National League West with an eye toward a playoff matchup. But the Cardinals' manager, Whitey Herzog, did not see the Braves' starting pitching as a huge threat to the Braves winning their division. "They can beat you in so many ways that I've got to think they're going to win the division," said Whitey Herzog. "They're too good."

The Braves stumbled into Atlanta on August 5 rolling out Pascual Perez against Fernando Valenzuela in front of almost 50,000 fans. For Perez, it was his second start of the season for the Braves, with his previous start also against Valenzuela on July 31 in Atlanta. Perez lost that game by pitching five innings and giving up three runs. Valenzuela pitched a 3-0 shutout, but Perez would get the better of Valenzuela in Los Angeles.

Pascual Perez and Fernando Valenzuela traded zeroes on the scoreboard while only allowing a combined three hits until the bottom of the fifth. Fernando Valenzuela induced a flyball to Rafael Ramirez for the first out of the inning, before walking the ninth batter, Pascual Perez. With a man on base, Claudell Washington struck a home run to right field and a 2-0 lead over the Dodgers.

The Braves ran off Valenzuela in the top of the sixth, with Bob Horner leading off the inning and Dodgers manager Tommy Lasorda going to the bullpen for Tom Niedenfuer.

It was now up to Pascual Perez to do what Joe Torre wanted from his starting pitchers, that is, pitch deep into the game handing the bullpen the lead. Perez worked around singles from Ron Cey and Bill Russell in the bottom of the fifth, before letting an unearned run across in the sixth inning on a Dusty Baker sacrifice fly bringing in Steve Sax and tightening the game to 2-1 Braves.

Pascual Perez and Tom Niedenfuer both did what was expected as they worked the game forward to the ninth inning without giving up a run. The ninth inning had both teams scramble for their top arm out of the bullpen—Steve Howe of the Dodgers to hold the Braves and Gene Garber of the Braves to nail down the Dodgers. This was going to be a battle of two good relievers who were both in the best year of their careers. For Howe, it would be the first of three games straight against the Braves in the series. The Braves would also lean on Garber three times in the four-game series.

Howe came out for the top of the ninth and put the Braves down in order. If Garber could do the same, the Braves would win.

Pedro Guerrero immediately put the Braves' win in jeopardy by leading the bottom of the ninth with a single to center field. The Dodgers, playing small ball with their power-hitting third baseman, Ron Cey, put down a sacrifice bunt moving Guerrero to second base for the first out. The usually dependable Steve Garvey popped up in foul territory for the second out of the inning leaving Guerrero stranded at second base. Rick Monday came up and hit a flyball to right fielder Claudell Washington that he could not handle, causing Guerrero to score on an error to tie the game at 2–2. Gene Garber then surrendered a hit to Mike Scioscia pushing Monday to third base. Scioscia took second base on defensive indifference setting up pinch hitter Ron Roenicke for the chance to win the game with a base hit. Roenicke was not able to capitalize as he hit a flyball to left field for the out.

The Braves were going to the top of the 10th inning with their bats on silent mode. The last Braves hit had been a Bob Horner base hit against Fernando Valenzuela to lead off the sixth inning. Reliever Terry Forster came in and shut down the Braves with three up and three down for the 15th consecutive out since chasing Fernando Valenzuela out of the game in the sixth inning.

Forster would later provide three excellent seasons for the Braves out of the bullpen during the 1983–1985 seasons.

Steve Sax led off an inning with a base hit again, but Claudell Washington made an error on the play allowing Sax to advance to second base. The Dodgers were looking to push the run across in any way possible, and they used a sacrifice bunt by Ken Landreaux to push Sax to third base with one out, an obvious sacrifice situation for the veteran Dusty Baker.

Joe Torre and the Braves then intentionally walked Dusty Baker and Pedro Guerrero to set up a bases-loaded with one out for Dodgers third baseman Ron Cey. The tactic was a solid strategy as Ron Cey, although a dangerous hitter, was slow-footed and a ground ball could be converted to a double play allowing the Braves to stay alive for the next inning. Ron Cey had already grounded into double plays twice to the Braves in 1982, on the way to his six against the Braves that year. Cey's six grounds into double play (GIDP) against the Braves were the most he had against any team that year, and the Braves had been able to convert double plays from Cey during back-to-back games on June 22 and 23.

That is the rub about baseball strategy; for Joe Torre it was not an analytical spreadsheet, it was a reasonable risk to have Gene Garber go for a groundout, or a ball kept to the infield versus a base hit or a sacrifice fly.

Ron Cey foiled the Braves' plans by lifting a ball to centerfield for a sacrifice fly scoring Steve Sax for their 59th win and placing them just three games behind the Braves in wins. The night was an unlucky night for Garber as he recorded his fifth blown save and took the loss bringing his record to 6–6. In fact, Garber was in the middle of a bad stretch lasting almost a month. From July 7 to August 5 he was scored on during 8 of 10 appearances, allowing 12 earned runs with his ERA increasing significantly from 1.46 to 2.70. Garber would continue to struggle through August with an ERA of 4.50 with opponents hitting .337 for the month before turning in a sparkling 1.11 ERA and a .191 batting average for September and October.

The next game started with Phil Niekro on the mound against Dave Stewart. Niekro pitched seven innings, surrendering nine base hits but limiting the Dodgers' bats to just three runs. Dave Stewart more than answered for the Dodgers with 7 1/3 innings of three-hit ball, with just a solo home run to pinch hitter Larry Whisenton before giving way to Steve Howe in the top of the eighth inning. Howe received a rude welcome into the game by the Braves as Claudell Washington singled to left field, Glenn Hubbard doubled to left field to score Washington from first, and Terry Harper drove Hubbard across to tie the game at 3–3. Like Garber the night before, Howe would be given a blown save for the night.

The Braves placed Steve Bedrosian in the game for Phil Niekro for the bottom of the eighth inning not allowing a run. Steve Howe and the Dodgers put the Braves down in order during the top of the ninth inning. The battle continued as Bedrosian was able to hold the Dodgers scoreless in the bottom of the ninth to send the game into extra innings.

Claudell Washington appeared to be an extra-innings hero by blasting a home run for the Braves to make it 4–3 for the Braves going into the bottom of the 10th with Bedrosian going out for his third inning of relief and looking to close out the game for the Braves' win.

A quick Dodgers fly ball by pinch hitter Jorge Orta made it one out with Ron Cey coming up to the plate. Cey hit a ground ball that the Braves wanted the previous night in extra innings, but this one was an error by Chris Chambliss at first base. Steve Garvey with a ground ball to shortstop went for the second out of the inning but was able to put Cey in scoring position at second base.

With the two outs and Cey on second, the game was still winnable for the Braves with the light-hitting Bill Russell coming up to the plate. Russell was batting under .250 for the year so far and already had two base hits. He had had a single and a double against the slow throwing Phil Niekro earlier in the game. Could he get good wood on a hard thrower like Steve Bedrosian?

Of course, Russell hit a single to score Cey from second base tying the game at 4–4. Scioscia followed with a single, and Bedrosian surrendered a walk to Roenicke to load the bases for Steve Sax. The Dodgers were able to walk-off another victory as Sax hit a ground ball to the shortstop Rafael Ramirez for an error, scoring Russell for the Dodgers' 60th win of the year. The Dodgers were just two wins behind the Braves in the NL West.

The Braves now had six errors against the Dodgers in just two games so far during the four-game series. Just as harmful were Bob Horner and Dale Murphy, with a combined two hits in 17 at-bats during the two games and no RBIs.

The next game turned out to be another crazy Saturday night in Los Angeles for the Braves, but with a repeated result. The starting pitchers were Bob Walk of the Braves versus Jerry Reuss of the Dodgers. Walk and Reuss managed to keep the game scoreless until the Braves broke through in the top of the fifth inning. A Jerry Royster base hit and ensuing balk placed him in scoring position for the pitcher, Bob Walk, to help his cause.

Pitchers are not known for skills with the bat, and Bob Walk batting in ninth spot was not a particularly a good hitter, but for a pitcher he wasn't an automatic out. His batting average in 1982 was right around the Mendoza line of a .200 batting average with 10 base hits in 51 at-bats, but he did squeeze out 10 walks and six RBIs. Walk took a pitch from Jerry Reuss and placed it into center field to bring home Royster from second base and a 1–0 lead. The hit was his fourth base hit in nine at-bats and his third straight game with an RBI and a base hit. Walk was outhitting the recently cold thunderous duo of Horner and Murphy.

Maybe the Dodgers should have walked Walk to get to the next batter, Rafael Ramirez, who hit a flyball stranding Walk in scoring position at second base. Ramirez finished his night 0–6 with only one hit in his last 21 at-bats.

As quickly as Bob Walk helped to take the lead at 1–0, he gave it right back in the bottom of the fifth inning by allowing a home run to Ron Cey and knotting the score at 1–1. Walk faced trouble when he loaded the bases with two outs and faced Ken Landreaux. Walk struck out Landreaux to end the threat and kept the score tied.

The Braves managed to lengthen the lead in the top of the sixth inning to 3–1 with two runs from two hits and an error, before Jerry Reuss was pulled for Tom Niedenfuer.

In the bottom of the sixth, Bob Walk found himself in quick trouble by giving up a double to Dusty Baker, and singles by Pedro Guerrero, and the now hot-hitting Ron Cey, bringing the Dodgers within one run and knocking Walk from the game with no outs in favor of Rick Mahler.

Mahler came in with two runners and Steve Garvey coming to bat. Garvey singled to load the bases, setting up a single to Bill Russell scoring Pedro Guerrero and tying the game at 3–3. With the bases still loaded and no outs, Mahler began to settle in, getting Mike Scioscia to pop-up and striking out pinch hitter Rick Monday. Mahler was done for the day after the next batter, Steve Sax, hit a single to bring in Garvey and Cey for a 5–3 Dodgers lead.

The Braves turned to Al "The Mad Hungarian" Hrabosky to replace Mahler and face Ken Landreaux. Hrabosky was popular during his 13-year playing career for his "Mad Hungarian" routine of turning his back to the plate before each batter while pounding his glove with the ball, stomping his feet, and actively trying to fire himself up for the pitcher-batter showdown. Hrabosky relished the drama of his routine, much like a professional wrestler whipping up the crowd. "When I'm on the road, my greatest ambition is to get a standing boo," explained Hrabosky. He retired Landreaux with a flyball to center field to end the bleeding for the Braves, who were trailing the Dodgers 5–3.

There were not many more encounters for Hrabosky. He only pitched a few more times, last being used on August 18, receiving his release from the Braves, and eventually retiring with a fine 13-year career and remembered as one of the best relievers of the 1970s.

When Al Hrabosky was released from the Braves, he understood the thinking behind the decision. "I have to feel it's the right move for the club, and I respect them for making it," Hrabosky said. "It is tough to win a pennant with 10 pitchers and 25 guys," explained Hrabosky as he was released on August 30.

The only regret he felt was for Ted Turner after seeing his ERA climb from 1.06 in 1981 to 5.54 in 1982. "The only thing I regret is that I let down the best owner in baseball, Ted Turner. I also let down my teammates, myself, the fans, and everybody else, but I keep thinking I let Ted down," said Hrabosky. "I really respect Ted for making this decision. Maybe I respect him more now than ever."

Almost every ball player will continue playing until someone asks them to wear their uniform for the last time, and for Hrabosky it would be no different. He could feel his end coming for the Braves. "I knew this would happen; I just didn't know when. I've been around long enough to read between the lines."

Joe Torre the consummate player manager said at the time of the difficult release, "He made it easier on me than I had any reason to expect."

The Braves and Dodgers were now in a tight division race, and it was being handled by Torre and Lasorda accordingly. The third game of the series was being managed like a World Series game with a bullpen game being utilized freely to maximize the matchups. Over the course of the game both teams took the gloves off their bullpen. The Braves would use six pitchers and the Dodgers five.

In 1982 pitching staffs were not nearly as deep as they are in present-day Major League Baseball. The staffs of the early 1980s were usually at 10 or 11 pitchers, whereas today a team can carry up to 13 pitchers on the game roster, and after August 31, 14 pitchers are allowed.

Terry Forster came into the game to relieve Tom Niedenfuer at the top of the seventh against the Braves. Forster made quick work of Rufino Linares and Rafael Ramirez for two outs before running into trouble with a Glenn Hubbard single, and an error allowed Hubbard to make it to third base. Dale Murphy stepped up to the dish with two outs and a runner needing to be brought home. Murphy showed signs of breaking out of his Dodgers slump with a double in the first inning off Jerry Reuss. In the seventh, Murphy delivered with an RBI single to center field scoring Hubbard and closing the deficit to 5–4.

Joe Torre placed Joe Cowley in the game for the bottom of the seventh inning as the fourth pitcher in the game since the start of the bottom of the sixth for the Braves. Cowley surrendered a home run to Pedro Guerrero making the score 6-4 in favor of the Dodgers. Then Forster and Cowley exchanged scoreless frames for the eighth inning, and the ninth began with Steve Howe pitching for the Dodgers and looking for the save.

No team wants errors in a game, especially when playing from ahead in the ninth inning. Bill Russell mishandled a ground ball from Bruce Benedict and followed it up with a throwing error to first base to bring Benedict to second base. Two quick outs of Chris Chambliss and Rafael Ramirez set Steve Howe just one out from the win as Glenn Hubbard dug in for his at-bat.

Glenn Hubbard smacked a double to left field scoring Benedict, making the score 5-4 with the National League leader in RBIs coming to the plate. Dale Murphy looked like he was back in hitting form and cracked a single to score Hubbard and tie the score at 6-6. Bob Horner grounded out for the third out, but the damage was done as the Braves scored twice with two hits and two errors.

Just like the Dodgers had done, the Braves brought in their closer. Gene Garber took the mound for the bottom of the ninth. Garber immediately allowed a single from Steve Sax, compounding the situation himself by throwing the ball away at first base to bring Sax to second with no outs. The Dodgers were once again going to attempt to manage the game tightly by using the small ball baseball fundamentals of scratching out a run and hopefully bringing Sax home for their third straight walk-off victory.

Ken Landreaux, using a sacrifice bunt, moved Sax to third base with no outs. Joe Torre knew exactly what to do; he had the script from a couple of nights back. It hadn't worked then, but hey, you never know. For Gene Garber it was déjà vu.

Joe Torre and the Braves intentionally walked Dusty Baker and Pedro Guerrero to set up a bases-loaded with one out for Dodgers third baseman Ron Cey. The solid tactic had backfired against the Braves two nights before when Cey hit a sacrifice fly winning the game. Now with the bases loaded and Garber against Cey again, this time Hubbard won the matchup striking out Cey, but Garber still had to get through the clutch-hitting former MVP, Steve Garvey, to keep hope alive by making it to extra innings. And Garber got Garvey to fly out to center field to save the inning.

Joe Beckwith became the fifth Dodgers pitcher of the night and put the Braves down in order in the top of the tenth inning. Garber shut down the Dodgers in the bottom of the tenth, only allowing a leadoff base hit by Bill Russell, before retiring the next three batters.

Beckwith did the same for the top of the eleventh, allowing a leadoff base hit to Bruce Benedict before retiring the next three batters in order.

Steve Bedrosian came in as the Braves sixth and final pitcher of the night for the bottom of the eleventh inning. Ken Landreaux struck out as the first batter, and Dusty Baker came up next to single and stole second base to move into scoring position for Pedro Guerrero. A flyball moved Baker to third base for pinch hitter Mike Marshall to drive in with a single to left field. The Dodgers walked it off again for the victory—three in as many games.

The Dodgers were just a game behind the Braves in the win column and were there in the most heartbreaking fashion for the Braves. The four-game debacle of a series would mercifully end after the next game. The Braves were not able to come off the mat after the three walk-off losses.

The Dodgers put Bob Welch on the mound, and the Braves countered with Rick Camp. Both pitchers were throwing marbles to the opposing batters with neither team putting up much offense. But the Dodgers had all they needed with a first-inning Pedro Guerrero RBI. Camp and Garber were able to hold the Dodgers to a series-low two runs, but Welch and Tom Niedenfuer allowed no runs to shut the Braves out 2–0. The Dodgers had pulled off the remarkable against a seemingly remarkable team.

By 1982, Tommy Lasorda was a baseball lifer of almost 40 years. His career had begun in 1945 when he was signed as an amateur free agent with the

Philadelphia Phillies organization. As a minor league pitcher, he struck out 25 batters in a 15-inning game in 1948 and made his MLB debut for the Dodgers in 1954. Lasorda even once played in AAA for the Yankees. After his longtime professional playing career ended after having appeared in just 26 major league games, he was hired as scout for the Dodgers in 1960 before working his way through the Dodgers organization eventually serving as a minor league manager and major league coach, before being named as the Dodgers skipper in 1976. Lasorda thought he had seen it all.

"I've never seen a team gain so much ground in a short period, not even in the minor leagues," explained Tommy Lasorda after the Dodgers took the four games at Dodgers Stadium. As the Dodgers were positioned squarely at the Braves heels, only 1 1/2 games behind in the National League West standings, Lasorda was beaming with pride. "There is nothing more exciting than being 10 1/2 games behind and looking up 10 days later and seeing yourself 1 1/2 games behind. It has to be the greatest heist since the Brinks Express robbery," explained Lasorda of their comeback.

The victories in Atlanta gave the Dodgers momentum going into their series at home against the Braves. The Dodgers were thinking they could play winning baseball after an inconsistent season to date. The Dodgers' Steve Garvey summed up how he felt around July 30 through the next 10 days. "We got it going at last, if we keep this going another two weeks, we'll be near the top," said Garvey. "We got pitching when we needed it, we were able to come from behind, we got the long ball, we got singles, we got the plays. What we did was play good quality baseball," explained Garvey on why the Dodgers beat the Braves eight straight times to close the gap in the standings.

Joe Torre remained a voice of reason in the clubhouse even as chaos could have broken the young team. "It's too early now to panic, just as it was too early to pop champagne on July 30," said Torre, referring to when the Braves led the Padres by nine games and the Dodgers by 10 1/2 games.

The Braves were reeling as they made it up the California coast to play the San Francisco Giants on August 9. Although the Braves held a slim lead over the Dodgers and Padres, the Giants were beginning to look like they could be trouble for the skidding Braves.

The Giants were not supposed to have been a worry for the Atlanta Braves on this road trip. Just as July 30 would have been too early for Joe Torre and the Braves to think they had wrapped up the National League West, it was too early for the Giants to mail in their season. The San Francisco team had seemed like little more than an afterthought to the Braves on July 30 as the Giants were at their low water mark of 13 1/2 games behind the Braves.

But as the Dodgers began to take chunks out of the Braves National League West lead, the Giants began to win too. They won eight out of nine games and were now just a handful of games out of the top spot in the suddenly competitive NL West along with the Braves, Dodgers, and Padres all in the playoff picture.

Pascual Perez took the bump for the Braves against Jim Barr of the Giants for some Monday night baseball. Perez was making his third straight start, pitching well and throwing seven innings, only allowing two earned runs. But the Giants made quick work of the Braves in a game of just 2 hours and 9 minutes, as Barr pitched a complete-game shutout allowing just three hits, all singles.

The Jim Barr gem left the Braves clinging to just half a game lead against a Dodgers team that was refusing to give up another inch. The Dodgers pulled off a fourth walk-off victory in their last five games (this time with the Cincinnati Reds) as Pedro Guerrero blasted his 22nd home run of the season in the bottom of the 13th inning to beat the Reds 3–2.

The next game between the Braves and the Giants was on August 10 and could be the one to knock Atlanta out of first place. Rick Mahler against Bill Laskey, a talented rookie pitcher who went 13–12 with a 3.14 ERA for the Giants in 1982 were the starting pitchers. Dale Murphy greeted Laskey rudely with a first inning home run to left field powering the Braves out to a quick 2–0 lead against the Giants. Laskey settled in after Murphy's blast shutting down the Braves bats with just five more base hits and not allowing another run through nine innings.

A solo home run by the Giants Milt May against Al Hrabrosky in the bottom of the seventh inning was the deciding run in the 3–2 game as Bob Horner, pinch-hitting for Bruce Benedict, struck out and ended the game for the Braves loss.

As Laskey and Mahler were taking the mound in what turned out to be a 3–2 pitcher's duel, the Dodgers and Reds were also about to face off. Reigning 1981 Cy Young Award–winning pitcher Fernando Valenzuela was facing Tom Seaver who already had three Cy Young Awards in his Hall of Fame career and was second to Valenzuela in 1981, after going 14–2 and leading the league in victories.

It was a marquee match-up that did not deliver a tight game with the Dodgers clobbering the Reds 11–3 for an easy win and taking sole possession of the National League West lead away from the Atlanta Braves for the first time all season.

The Braves lost ground in the standings lead more rapidly than the infamous historical collapses of the 1951 Dodgers, 1964 Phillies, 1969 Cubs, or 1978 Red Sox. Were the 1982 Braves going to be an afterthought, a footnote in history after such a breathtaking start to the season?

From July 30 until August 10 the collapse was a team effort. Bad pitching, horrific hitting, and erratic fielding all showed themselves and often all in the same games and led to an epic fall in the National League West standings.

During the 13-game, 12-loss stretch, the Braves had a team batting average of just .194. A great hitter can often carry a team and lead them through a rough patch, but the Braves' two great hitters both went into slumps at this time. Bob Horner only drove in six RBIs, and Dale Murphy went 8–52, with 12 games without a home run.

The Braves committed 20 errors in the 13-game span, and they were not able to produce double plays as they normally had been doing all season. The Braves middle infielders were only able to generate three double plays during the skid.

The normally superb Braves bullpen made 21 appearances allowing runs to score in 15 of the appearances for a collective 0–8 win-loss and 6.02 ERA.

After the August 10 Braves 3–2 loss to the Giants, Torre was upset about falling out of first place for the first time in 104 days. "Hopefully, it's temporary, and hopefully it will get some people mad, it's time to look at the standings and take back what we feel rightfully belongs to us," said a defiant Joe Torre. It would be another two weeks before the Braves would be able to get back into first place.

On August 11, Phil Niekro took the ball for the last game in San Francisco, allowing just one earned run in 5 2/3 innings pitched. Two errors and a passed ball kept the Giants in the game with the score 6–6 from the bottom of the seventh inning all the way until a bottom of the 12th home run by Jeffrey Leonard put the Giants over the top for the win. With the Reds beating the Dodgers 2–1, the Braves remained half a game behind the Dodgers, but the Giants gained a game on the Dodgers to be just four games behind the Dodgers and 3 1/2 behind the Braves.

The Giants would continue to thrust themselves into the NL West title run, and before it was over, the Giants would help to keep the Dodgers from pulling too far ahead as the Braves remained mired in the throes of a losing streak and the glares of fans thinking that removing Chief Noc-A-Homa's tepee was somehow contributing to the colossal drop in the team's good fortune.

The Braves' dreadful road trip was still not over, as now they had to trudge back to Southern California to face the still contending San Diego Padres for four games. The Braves did not show much left in their tank as they lost three of four games and were outscored 26–16 by the Padres. But there were some good signs as the Braves snapped their 11-game losing streak with a 6–5 come-from-behind victory during the third game of the series before returning the favor losing 6–5 the next game to the Padres to close their road trip.

Traditionally, baseball is a game full of superstitions, like not mentioning a no-hitter while in progress or even talking to the pitcher during that time, not stepping on the foul line chalk, or making sure to eat the same meal if on a hitting streak. When the Braves were on a winning streak, it was initially not seen as a big deal to remove the Chief-Noc-A-Homa area for extra seating capacity. But as the team started to lose games and lose ground in the National League West standings, the superstitious Braves fans began to mount pressure on the Braves as the fans felt the team was somehow cursed for removing the seats. Braves fans started an outcry to bring back the Chief, and finally Ted Turner agreed to set the tepee back up. "The general public was saying it was because we took the tepee down that we lost," Chief-Noc-A-Homa said. "There were people who came to the stadium wearing tepees on top of their head, and it was the general public's outcry that finally caused Ted Turner to put the tepee back up."

As the Braves were snapping their 11-game losing streak in San Diego on August 14, the Atlanta Falcons football fans sitting in the converted Chief-Noc-A-Homa section at Atlanta-Fulton County Stadium were watching the Falcons beat the Minnesota Vikings 20–17. Stadiums that were shared by NFL and MLB teams often deferred to the NFL teams' wishes for the stadium configuration, but in this case, the Braves held the field preference.

The fact that the Braves played at home on grass instead of carpet over concrete was certainly rare; from 1970 until 1990, only one new Major League Baseball stadium had been built with a grass field, the Arlington Stadium, in Texas. Atlanta-Fulton County stadium was built with football in mind (as a dual-stadium), but it opened when artificial field surfaces were in their infancy as the miracle playing turf was thought to be more efficient and more long-term economically feasible.

Braves baseball fans were blessed to see baseball and football games on grass, but now Braves fans were demanding that football not take their Chief-Noc-A-Homa seats back. The fans' voices and their superstitions finally swayed the Braves to bring back the tepee.

Even as the Braves agreed to bring back the Chief, the modifications would not be concluded until after the Montreal Expos mid-week series at home in Atlanta. The Braves would have to get through the four-game set without more bloodshed before an anticipated larger weekend crowd versus the Mets.

The Braves were routed over the first three games against the Expos losing a combined 28–11. After the third loss in a row to the Expos, the Braves sunk all the way back to fifth place in the NL standings behind the Saint Louis Cardinals, Philadelphia Phillies, Los Angeles Dodgers, and the Montreal Expos. They were bleeding out runs against their opponents at an alarming 515 runs, the worst at that point in the National League West.

Phil Niekro took an unexpected Thursday night start hoping to avoid the sweep by the Expos in front of 12,205 fans on August 19. The previous night's 12–2 shellacking didn't provide a lot of hope, but the knuckleballer did just well enough to win the game, as the Expos Gary Carter and Tim Wallach both hit a two-run home run to make it a tight 5–4 Braves victory. The reason why Niekro had to start that night was later credited as one of the turning points of the Braves season.

The 1982 New York Mets were not a good team, which could be exactly what was needed for the Braves to snap out of their August doldrums. But this was not the ferocious Braves team tearing up the National League and pacing Major League Baseball as they had been earlier in the year.

The dog days of August often expose the flaws of young teams and separate the pretenders from the contenders. Were the Braves a contending team of blooming talent or a young pretending team playing above their heads for a new manager during a nice run? Did the "kids" and Joe Torre have it in them to persevere through adversity? Teams can only play the teams on their schedule, and on paper, the Mets looked like an easy win for a team trying to be a contender.

The Mets were just 5–13 for August as they rolled into Atlanta-Fulton County Stadium, but somehow the Braves were even worse at 3–16 for the month of August. The Braves were going the wrong way, but this turned around after a player (one of the Braves own) took the wrong way to the stadium and got lost, like really lost. Seriously.

The box score of the August 20 game showed "lots of strange," as a huge increase in fans from 12,205 on Thursday to a Friday-night crowd with Chief Noc-A-Homa in attendance swelled the crowd to 33,144 fans. Calendars can be set to which pitcher is going to start which night, and the fact that Pascual Perez and Phil Niekro traded nights is one of the most infamous stories in baseball lore.

Perez was supposed to start the game on August 19 against the Expos, and Niekro was scheduled as the August 20 starting pitcher against the Mets. But as fans settled into their seats for the closing game against the Expos, it was Niekro warming up in the bullpen for the start with no Perez in sight. Perez was trapped in the middle of two or three laps around the stadium on the I-285 highway, not sure how to exit the beltway and get to the stadium. Each lap meant having to go around the entire perimeter of the city of Atlanta. By the time Perez's journey was complete, it had taken almost 3 1/2 hours to make what would normally be a 10-minute ride.

As time moved forward with no starting pitcher in sight, the Braves began to fear the worst and notified law enforcement to look out for Perez in case he had been in a car accident or had gotten in some kind of trouble. But the Dominican Republic–born Perez had just received his license that day and was unfamiliar with the roads; to make things even worse, he had left his wallet at home. Each loop around the city lowered the rental car's gas tank leaving Perez with the real threat of being stranded on the highway with no means of getting to the stadium for his start. Perez stopped three times for directions and borrowed $10 for gas before finally getting to the stadium 10 minutes after Niekro threw the first pitch of the game.

Years later during an interview with *Sports Illustrated*'s Frank Lidz, Pascual Perez provided this account in his second language, English.

There's a big radio, and the merengue music was real loud.... I forgot my wallet, so I have no money and no license. I pass around the city two times easy, but the car so hot, I stop at a gas station. I ask for $10 worth, and the guy say, 'You Pascual Perez? People been waiting for you at the stadium.' I'm 20 minutes away, he tells me. I feel like a heart attack. I think I get fired, maybe. Boss Torre say he fine me $100. I say, 'What you say, $100?' He smile, say, 'Ciento pesos.' I smile. Ciento pesos worth only 10 bucks.

"Perimeter Pascual" Perez found his way to the stadium the next night to face the Mets. "Easy getting here today. Easy, easy," Perez told reporters after the game. "I follow map. I got on I-85, not I-285, and it took about 15 minutes. I know the way now."

The fans were not treated to a huge display of offensive output as the Mets Ed Lynch shut down the Braves allowing six hits through nine innings. Perez countered by also pitching nine scoreless frames, allowing seven hits through his nine innings. It was a 0–0 game going into some free extra baseball for the fans.

Torre decided to keep with Perez for the top of the 10th inning against the Mets' 8-9-1 hitters in the lineup.

Perez found instant trouble with the first batter in the top of 10th inning as Mets rookie, Brian Giles, hit his first ML home run to put the Mets in the lead 1–0. Perez battled back to strike out the pinch-hitting George Foster, and then inducing a groundout of Bob Bailor to first base for the second out of the inning. Rusty Staub proved he still had life in his bat, as the 38-year-old belted a double to place himself on second furthering the Mets threat and knocking Perez out of the game in favor of Steve Bedrosian. Perez received a standing ovation for his delayed start, but more so for his 9 2/3 shutout innings. Ellis Valentine ended the threat by grounding out to end the top of the 10th.

The Mets countered by sending Pat Zachry to face the Braves' 7-8-9 hitters. The Pat Zachry story is one of highs and lows. He was the NL Rookie of the Year in 1976 for the Cincinnati Reds and was held in such high regard that he was the centerpiece of the 1977 trade of Tom Seaver away from the Mets to the Reds. The Mets were quickly rewarded for their confidence as Zachry made the All-Star Team as a Met in 1978, but he was no longer of that caliber four years later.

The 1982 Mets manager was George Bamberger who had a view of pitching that is counter to the standards of today. Bamberger was a long-time former minor league pitcher winning 213 games and pitching 3,277 innings across 18 minor league seasons. Bamberger did play briefly for the New York Giants and the Baltimore Orioles, pitching in 10 games, 14 1/3 innings against 25 hits with a 9.42 ERA. He threw a lot of innings as a minor league pitcher, and he believed the way to avoid a sore arm was to work it more. Simply put, a sore armed pitcher would have to throw more to avoid injury.

Two days after a start, Bamberger's pitchers would do 20 minutes of hard throwing in the bullpen. In the case of Zachry, it would be to face the Braves in the bottom of the 10th after going 7 1/3 innings, while having given up 10 hits to his former team, the Cincinnati Reds, just two nights before on August 18. George Bamberger as the pitching coach for the 1970 Baltimore Orioles used the "overwork" strategy to great success as the team won the World Series with his top three starting pitchers taking the ball every four days.

Bamberger believed in pitchers throwing many innings and completing as many starts as they could. In 1970, Jim Palmer, Mike Cuellar, and Dave McNally each pitched approximately 300 innings for the year, with all placing in the top-five in the Cy Young Award for top pitcher in the American League in 1970, while winning at least 20 games each. For Bamberger, the idea was to be efficient, trading wasted pitches for completed innings.

"My whole idea is to throw the ball over the plate," Bamberger told Dave Anderson of the *New York Times* in 1979. "The most important pitch is a strike. But the trick is to change speeds. Trying to pinpoint a pitch is crazy. Throw the ball down the middle, but don't throw the same pitch twice. Change the speed."

That strategy may have worked with a team constructed like the 1972 Orioles with perhaps the greatest defensive third baseman of all time in Brooks Robinson, the perennial Gold Glove Mark Belanger at shortstop, three-time Gold Glove winner Davey Johnson at second, and a surprisingly athletic Boog Powell at first base. The Mets were not that team, and Pat Zachry was not going to be one of those guys on the mound.

Joe Torre and George Bamberger were about to pull out the stops managing the bottom of the 10th.

Pat Zachry quickly sent pinch hitter Rufino Linares down with a fly ball to center field for the first out. Rafael Ramirez as the next batter slapped a double bringing Biff Pocoroba to pinch hit for the pitcher and drawing a walk. Matt Sinatro pinch ran for the slow-footed Pocoroba. It was now first and second, one out, with swift runners on base for Jerry Royster to hit. Royster delivered with a hit to left field for what looked like the tying run. Before the inning had started, George Bamberger moved the strong-armed Bob Bailor from shortstop to replace Rusty Staub in left field. Bailor was replaced at shortstop by the pinch running Ron Gardenhire who ran for Staub from the previous inning. Bailor came up with the throw from Royster's hit to nail Ramirez at home, thus preserving the 1–0 Mets lead.

Torre sent his third pinch hitter of the inning against Zachry with Terry Harper replacing left fielder Larry Whisenton in the batting lineup. With Matt Sinatro at second, and Royster on first, Harper hit a ground ball to Mets third baseman Hubie Brooks resulting in a throwing error to first base and allowing Sinatro to score tying the game at 1–1.

George Bamberger decided to intentionally walk Claudell Washington loading the bases against Dale Murphy, essentially betting that the eventual

1982 National League MVP and leader in RBIs for 1982, would not be able to bring home a runner with two outs against Pat Zachry. Murphy had had consecutive hits earlier that year off Zachry during his last start on May 24.

Until digging in for his bottom of the 10th, Murphy was 5 for 15, with a .333 batting average since 1976 against Zachry. Claudell Washington first appeared against Zachry in 1981 and went 3–7 in his at-bats against Zachry before the intentional walk. Murphy never received an intentional walk from Zachry in 33 plate appearances.

It would be clear that Zachry wanted soft contact for an easy out, or a much more likely strikeout against a strikeout prone Murphy. But in no way could Zachry just lay it down the middle hoping for a contact out.

Murphy was a patient hitter, with an aggressive swing resulting in the kind of batter who could lead the league in walks (1990), strikeouts (1978, 1980, and 1985), or RBIs (1982–1983). This at-bat for Murphy resulted in the favorable outcome of a walk to bring in the winning run and a walk-off 2–1 victory over the sinking Mets.

Looking back on the August 20 game, it is hard not to circle this as an important game, perhaps changing the trajectory of the season for the Braves. "It was Pascual Perez getting lost," said manager Joe Torre. "That made the players laugh and relax. And that turned us back around."

The Mets lost their next 11 games in August to finish the month at an embarrassing 5–24 win-loss record while the Braves had been 3–16 up to that point in August but were able to win 10 of the 12 remaining games during August to finish at 13–18. The Braves came into August with a seven-game lead in the National League West, and even with an 11-game losing streak, they managed to claw their way back to regain the National League West lead going into September 1 clinging to a 1/2 game lead over the Dodgers.

Up until that Dale Murphy walk, the Braves were three games behind the Dodgers and had a .536 winning percentage, good for second in the National League West and fourth in the National League. With the August 20 win, the

Braves went 24–17 with a .585 winning percentage over the remaining games, good for the most wins in the National League, and playing four games better than the Dodgers in the same span. The Braves began to hit again!

The Braves' 210 runs scored over their last 41 games also easily led the National League, outpacing the Dodgers who had a National League second-best with 172 during the same span. The bats came back covering up the warts of the pitching staff as the Braves also led the National League with "runs scored against" of 182 during the same span. For the rest of August, the Braves were going to have to gut through games for tight victories.

The August 20 win over the Mets started what would eventually be 12 wins over the next 14 games, and the Braves would need this as they finished the rest of September and October below .500 ball at 13–15 from September 4 through the end of the season, ensuring a below .500 second half of the season at 38–40.

The Braves were playing streaky, good and bad, while the Dodgers finished close to .500 for April at 10–11, following up May, June, and July with a winning record in each month before catching fire with a 19–10 win-loss record in August with a .655 winning percentage. It was a classic case of a veteran team understanding the long baseball season and how to be in the best position to play October baseball.

As the Braves floundered after 1969, the Los Angeles Dodgers flourished in 11 of the 12 previous years finishing in first or second place in the National League West, with 1979 being a substandard year with the Dodgers finishing third. The Braves during the same time frame did not finish higher than third. Simply put, the Dodgers were expecting to be there standing at the end, and the other team was expected to collapse.

The Braves, though, were playing like a young team, inconsistent with losing records for the months of May and August. They were hoping to stay ahead in the standings, but the veteran Dodgers squad seemed to be flipping the switch that the great teams seem to find down the stretch.

However, starting with the "Wrong Way Pascual" game on August 19, the Braves won five games in a row with each game at a one-run difference. The Braves swept the Mets over the three games to find themselves just a game out of the National League West standings.

The Philadelphia Phillies were coming into Atlanta with ill intentions and fighting for a playoff spot. The Phillies were a proud veteran team that had won the World Series over the Kansas City Royals in 1980 and lost in six games to the Baltimore Orioles in the 1983 World Series. The Phillies were in second place at just two games behind the Saint Louis Cardinals on August 23 and would soon briefly take over the top spot in the National League East standings, but they were playing so-so ball with a 5–5 record over their last 10 games and would finish 15–17 for the month of August.

The Braves had right-hander Rick Camp on the mound for the August 23 game looking for his first win of the month after going 0–3 in his four starts with his last start having been his worst of the season with 3 1/3 innings pitched and giving up six earned runs against the Montreal Expos on August 18.

The Phillies' righty, Mike Krukow, was able to match zeros on the scoreboard until the Braves broke through with two runs in the bottom of the fourth inning.

The Braves resorted to playing small ball after Jerry Royster led the inning with a base hit to left field off Mike Krukow. Rafael Ramirez pushed Royster to second base with a sacrifice bunt for the first out. Claudell Washington hit a single to center field to move Royster to third base. The table was set for Dale Murphy to bring in the runner from third as he singled Royster in for the 1–0 lead and his 89th RBI of the year. The next batter, Bob Horner, drove home the second run of the inning to make it 2–0 scoring Washington on a sacrifice fly.

The Phillies broke through in the top of the sixth after Pete Rose singled to left field starting off the inning and eventually scoring on a Mike Schmidt sacrifice fly tightening the Braves' lead to 2–1. The Braves took back the run during the bottom of the sixth inning as Washington hit a one-out hit to right field and stole second base before being knocked in by a hit to center field by Horner bringing the Braves to a 3–1 lead.

This lead would hold until the top of the eighth, when the Phillies Manny Trillo singled, and former Braves outfielder Gary Matthews homered to make it a 3–3 game. Then Phillies reliever Ed Farmer came in the game replacing Mike Krukow for the seventh and eighth innings and shutting the Braves down with three up, three down for each inning. Joe Torre kept Rick Camp on the mound for the ninth inning and was rewarded for his faith in his starting pitcher, as Camp managed to strand two men on base, giving the Braves bats a chance to go for a walk-off win in the bottom of the ninth.

Dale Murphy led off the ninth inning with a ground out, but Bob Horner continued his good night with a base hit. Torre once again pushed the right button by replacing Horner with the speedy pinch runner Brett Butler. Chris Chambliss came up in another crucial spot for the Braves and responded with a double to right field for a walk-off 4–3 Braves victory. The Braves were finally not behind the Dodgers in the standings for the first time in two weeks, and each game was about to feel more important for both teams who were fighting it out for the NL West title.

The arrival of Chambliss to play 1B allowed the Braves to shift Murphy to the outfield. Courtesy of Topps.

Dale Murphy as a MLB catcher was a work in progress, but his bat was too valuable to not be in the lineup. Courtesy of Topps.

Dale Murphy the Super Hero! Courtesy of Topps.

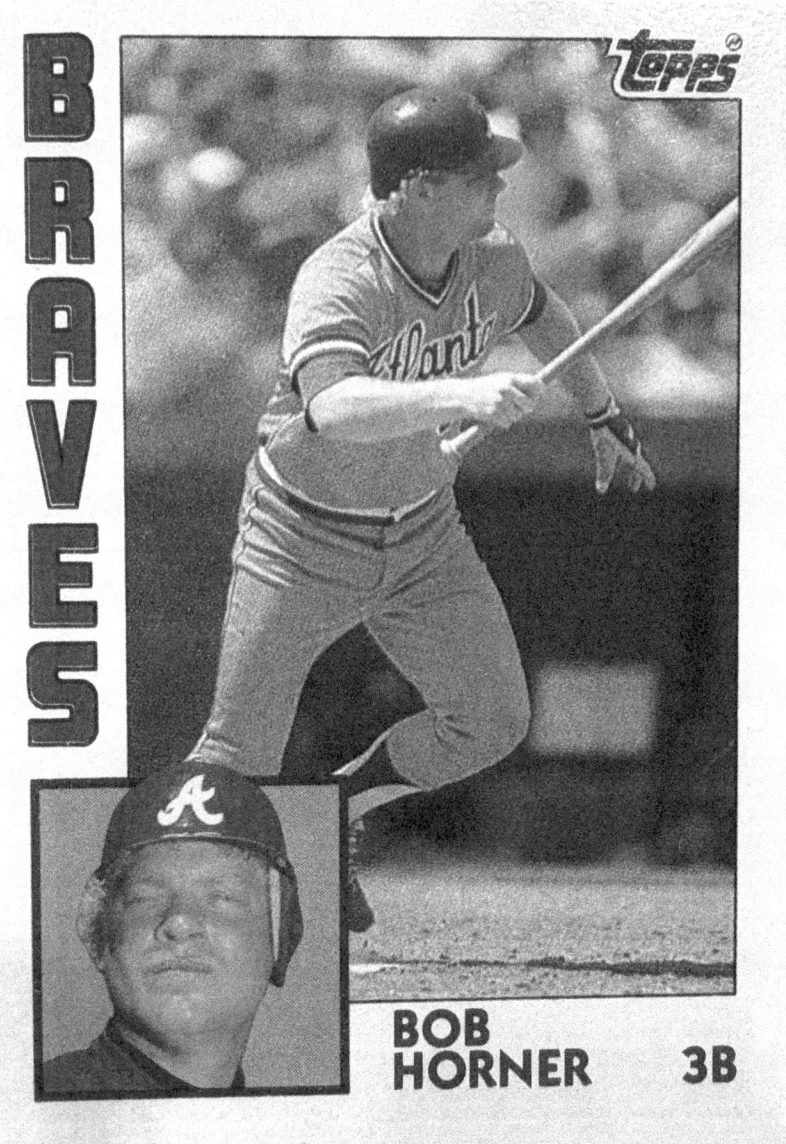

Horner and Murphy were a power tandem to hit the Braves into contention under Torre. Courtesy of Topps.

Joe Torre as a rookie for the Braves. Courtesy of Topps.

Niekro as a youngster for the Braves. Courtesy of Topps.

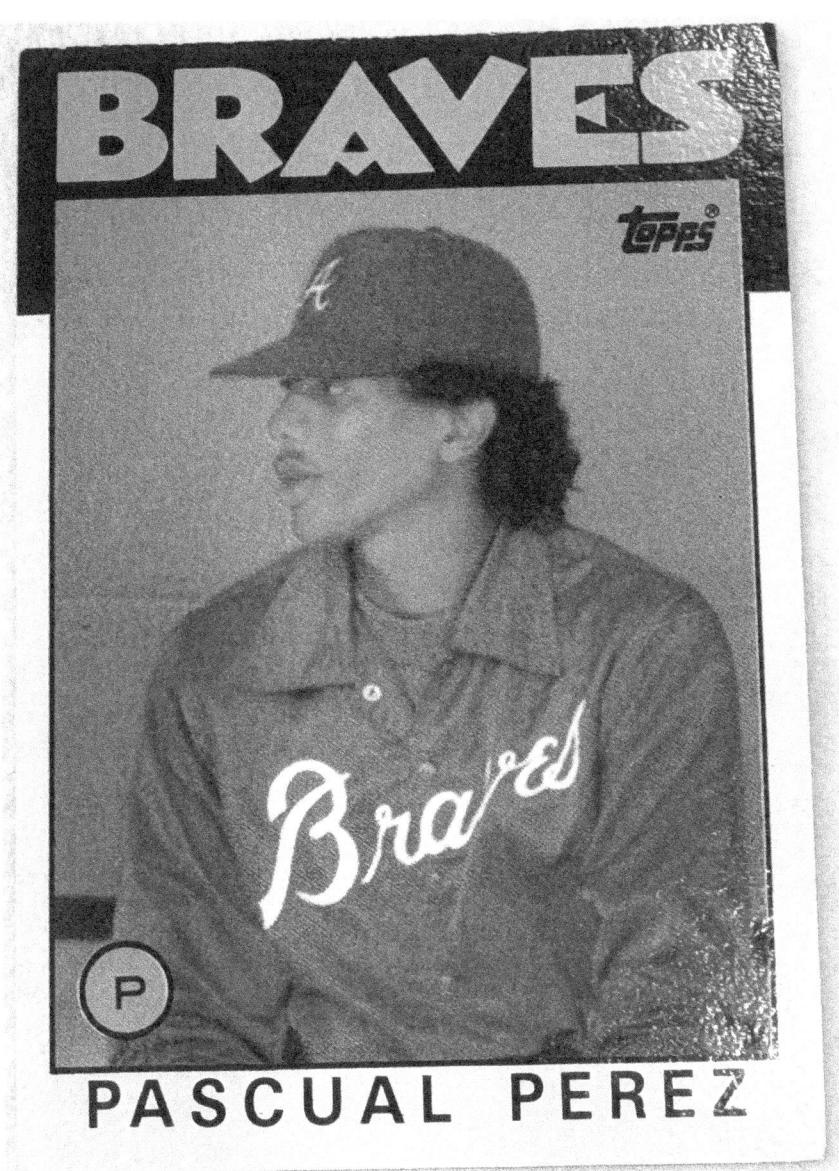

Perez and his navagational skills helped bring the 1982 season to a title. Courtesy of Topps.

In 1982, Joe Torre led the Braves to their first Division Title since 1969. Courtesy of Topps.

Bobby Wine replaced Eddie Haas in 1985 as Braves Manager. Courtesy of Topps.

6

The Chase

On August 23, the Braves celebrated both a walk-off victory as Brett Butler came across the plate for the win and being at the top of the National League West for the first time since August 9, with 14 games, as they were now tied with the Dodgers in the standings.

Back on August 19, the Braves had been four games behind the Dodgers when Pascual Perez was doing laps around Atlanta-Fulton County Stadium with Phil Niekro pressed into an early start, and now, five games later, on August 24, Niekro was on the mound again with the Braves having erased a four-game deficit in just five games. The Dodgers had lost four of their last five games, giving life to the Braves as Niekro took the mound for the Braves versus the Philadelphia Phillies' Steve Carlton. The game featured a Hall of Fame starting pitcher but was anything but a quality start for Niekro or Carlton.

Carlton was in his last All-Star season as a player, but it was one of his best as the 37-year-old lefty went 23–11, winning his fourth Cy Young award in 1982. But the night of August 24, Carlton was not at his best, allowing seven earned runs in 3 2/3 innings.

The Phillies tagged Niekro for a quick 4–0 lead in first inning. Carlton gave up a solo home run in the bottom of the first to Jerry Royster, and another solo shot in the bottom of the third, this time to Bob Horner, tightening the game at a 4–2 Phillies lead before a disastrous fourth inning for Carlton.

The Braves hit Carlton hard in the bottom of the fourth as they hit for a cycle against him in that inning. Carlton surrendered singles to Terry Harper and Rafael Ramirez, a double to Jerry Royster, a triple to Bruce Benedict, and a two-out home run to Dale Murphy to complete the fourth inning "Carlton Cycle."

Ed Farmer replacing Carlton still couldn't cool the Braves bats as they continued their fourth-inning onslaught with three straight hits, a double, and two singles for another run. Glenn Hubbard hit a flyball for the third out ending a string of six straight Braves batters with a base hit and an 8–4 Braves lead.

The Braves needed the four-run cushion as Niekro allowed three runs in the sixth inning after Ivan de Jesus belted a three-run home run closing the gap to 8–7 with the Braves still out front. Hubbard's single off the Phillies reliever Tug McGraw in the bottom of the sixth inning widened the lead to 9–7 for the Braves. Then Niekro shut down the Phillies in the seventh and eighth innings with three up, three down, and bringing confidence as Niekro took the mound at the bottom of the ninth, with a 9–7 lead looking to bring home the victory.

Joe Torre made changes to the defensive alignment for the Braves at the top of the ninth inning with Chris Chambliss taking first base for Bob Watson, Jerry Royster going to third base from left field, Dale Murphy changing to left field, and Brett Butler moving from pinch runner for Bob Horner to playing center field.

A leadoff single to Greg Gross by Niekro triggered a call to the Braves bullpen with Gene Garber now on the mound to face Pete Rose with a runner on first base. Garber won the matchup as Rose hit into a double play. Garber quickly ended the game as Manny Trillo grounded back to the pitcher for the third out and the 9–7 Braves victory.

Wins do not always mean movement in the standings, and it didn't that night as the Dodgers with Bob Welch held the Cardinals to just four base hits winning that game 5–2 for the Dodgers and remaining tied with the Braves in the standings. The Braves and Dodgers were answering each other as neither team would allow the other more than a one game lead throughout the next week.

Even though the Braves tied the Dodgers in the division lead on August 23 and went 7–2 from then to the end of August, this resulted in just a half game lead for the Braves in the National League West.

The Braves remained in at least a tie for first from August 23 until the San Francisco Giants beat the Braves 3–2 on September 7 briefly knocking the Braves to second place, half a game behind the Dodgers.

For the San Francisco Giants, it was their fifth straight victory, bringing the team a handful of games behind the leaders with a precious few weeks to go in the pennant chase, announcing a three-team stretch run for the title.

The Braves kept afloat by going 6–5 over the first 11 September games, having the division lead (as high as 2 1/2 games over the Dodgers) before a three-game sweep to the Houston Astros and a loss to the Cincinnati Reds finally gave the Dodgers the chance to separate from the Braves on September 17, by opening a 3 1/2 game cushion with just 15 games left in the season, and the Giants were 6 1/2 games behind.

But the Braves pitching was a cause of concern for Joe Torre and the team. "The pitching still worries me, it has all year, and we will go as far as it carries us," explained Joe Torre as the team was into their September stretch.

Once again it would fall upon the ageless Phil Niekro to help pull the Braves out of trouble, and he was going to have a little brotherly help while he was on the mound in Cincinnati. Niekro had his little brother, Joe Niekro, ready to help the Braves' cause by taking the mound against the Dodgers in Los Angeles.

The night of September 18, the Niekro brothers were both on the road armed with their knuckleball. For Phil, it was time to stop the Braves from slipping farther behind in the perilous National League West division race, and for brother Joe pitching for the Houston Astros, he was looking for another great outing during one of the best seasons of his underappreciated pitching career. Joe Niekro last pitched on September 13 winning 5–3 against the Braves in a game his brother started as well.

Joe Niekro was not originally a knuckleball pitcher like his brother. He made it to the big leagues through his fastball and slider combination, starting with the Chicago Cubs in 1967, and later pitching for the San Diego Padres and Detroit Tigers taking regular turns in the starting rotation. Joe joined Phil and the Braves in 1973 and 1974, in a brief union of the brothers.

Joe Niekro was not overly successful pitching for the Atlanta Braves with a 5–6 win-loss record and a 3.76 ERA over 67 innings. But Joe became reacquainted with the knuckleball pitch that both Phil and Joe had learned years earlier from their father. Phil was the greatest knuckleball pitcher in Major League Baseball history and tutored Joe on the pitch, breathing new life into his younger brother's career.

Joe's time in baseball pales in comparison to his older brother's Hall-of-Fame career, but for a 10-year run with the Astros, Joe was arguably just as good as brother Phil and among the finest pitchers in baseball. He placed in the top-five in National League Cy Young Award voting in 1979 and 1980, winning at least 20 games each year. In fact, Joe—with his 221 career wins over his 22 years in the big leagues—combined with Phil holds the major league record of 539 total wins by a pair of brothers.

Sibling "all-time lists" are dominated by Braves:

- Hank and Tommie Aaron of the Braves hold the all-time record for career home runs by a pair of brothers with 768 home runs.

- The brother combination of Justin and B. J. Upton, both playing for the Braves on April 23, 2023, hit back-to-back home runs the first time a pair of brothers had accomplished that feat since Lloyd and Paul Warner did so for the Pirates in 1938.

- On August 8, 2014, while playing for the Braves, Justin and B. J. Upton set an MLB record when they hit a home run in the same game for the fifth time, passing Vladimir and Wilton Guerrero and Jason and Jeremy Giambi.

On May 29, 1976, Joe Niekro hit the only big-league home run of his career (973 lifetime at-bats), and it came off his brother Phil. In the 1987 World Series with Minnesota, Joe set a record for the longest period between a major league debut (1967) and a first appearance in the series.

Even with Hall of Fame pitcher Nolan Ryan on the Houston Astros, Joe Niekro was probably the last Astros pitcher the Dodgers wanted to see on the mound. Joe had kept them scoreless through eight innings of the 1981 National League Divisional Series, and the Dodgers were held to one run through eight innings in Joe's other 1982 start against the Dodgers on April 12 during a 2–1 loss to the Astros.

Joe owned the Dodgers on September 18, 1982, as he pitched a complete game two-hit shutout for his 16th victory of the year. The pitching start was his best during his outstanding 17-win 1982 season and was the second of the three two-hit games of his career. The other two-hit games were against the San Francisco Giants in 1978 and later in 1985. Joe had a no-hit bid broken in the bottom of the eighth inning against the California Angels on June 4, 1986, as Gary Pettis hit a two-out double. Yankees manager Lou Piniella inserted reliever Al Holland for the 41-year-old Joe to preserve to an 11–0, one-hit victory for the Yankees.

Across the country in Cincinnati on September 18, Phil Niekro was trying to keep up with his younger brother, maybe not pitching as well as Joe, but ultimately good enough for the 5–4 win, and announcing the Braves were still to be reckoned with.

The top of the first inning started out badly for the Braves offense as both Claudell Washington and Jerry Royster made quick outs for Frank Pastore on the mound. But a walk to Dale Murphy opened the door for the Braves offense to lash out.

Five straight singles by the Braves pushed three runs across, leaving three men on base as Niekro grounded out to end the scoring. Niekro pitched six strong innings, scattering six hits and allowing two solo home runs to Reds infielder Ron Oester. Gene Garber came in to close the game with three innings pitched for his 28th save of the year and preserving the game for Niekro, bringing Niekro to a 15–4 record. The Braves were now on their way back in the National League West standings at 2 1/2 games back and were beginning a one-week climb to the top of the standings.

By 1982, Phil was 43 years old and a long way from his 1969 National League West Division Championship with the Atlanta Braves. As a 30-year-old, Niekro pitched to a 23–12 record with a 2.56 ERA, making his first All-Star Team and placing second in the National League Cy Young Award voting. He was given the honor of the Game 1 NLCS Starter for the Braves but took the 9–5 loss to Tom Seaver and the Mets as the Mets swept the NLCS 3–0 on their way to the 1969 World Series Championship against the heavily favored Baltimore Orioles. The Major League leading 109 wins for the Baltimore Orioles meant little as the Mets came back from a Game 1 loss to take the next four games winning the 1969 World Series in five games.

The 1969 season was Niekro's first sniff at the postseason, and he probably thought there would be others soon.

But Niekro suffered through a miserable 1970 season. He fell to 12 wins and a 4.27 ERA as the Braves slipped to a fifth-place finish of 76–86, 26 games behind in the National League West to the Cincinnati Reds. In fact, Niekro did not play with meaningful postseason hopes for over a decade, but now in 1982, he was going all out to get there. He was about to take the team on his 43-year-old body and drag them across the finish line.

Phil Niekro missed the first two weeks of the year with injury but finished the 1982 season like a man possessed. He went 3–0 in his last four starts totaling 30 innings pitched, allowing two earned runs and hurling back-to-back complete game shutouts to end the season.

A 6–1 win the next night by Pascual Perez in the third game tilted the series for the Braves as they took two of three games in Cincinnati on September 17–19. The Braves were about to roll into Houston against an inhospitable

Astros team that had just taken three in a row from the Braves in Atlanta. The Atlanta Braves owned the Houston Astros for most of the season going 10-2 until the Astros swept the September 13-15 games. Now the Astros were looking to take even more games from the Braves during the September 20-22 games, just as the Braves needed the wins the most.

The first game of the three-game series was a heartbreaker for the Atlanta Braves as they lost on a walk-off double by Dickie Thon in the bottom of the ninth inning off Gene Garber for the 4-3 loss. The Atlanta Braves also lost the next two games 5-3 and 3-2, but they did not lose ground in the standings as the Dodgers lost consecutive games to the San Diego Padres keeping the Braves at three games back. The Braves were about to travel home to open a three-game series on September 24 against the San Diego Padres and needed to avoid a similar fate at the hands of the Padres.

The Atlanta Braves were now down to their last ten games of the regular season and still a few games back going into their last homestand of the season. For the hometown fans, there was a real possibility that the Braves would fall out of playoff contention before the team would leave town for a brutal West Coast trip, playing the top three teams in the National League West.

The Los Angeles Dodgers would have a slightly more advantageous final 10-game schedule with seven of their games played at home, including two games against an inferior Cincinnati Reds team, with the five remaining home games against the Atlanta Braves and San Francisco Giants. The final three Dodgers games would be on the road in San Francisco against the Giants with the possibility that each game would be needed to wrap-up a return trip to the postseason to defend their 1981 World Series Championship.

How many games would the Atlanta Braves have to win of their last ten? How many could the Dodgers lose and still win the National League West? Were the San Francisco Giants at ten games back capable of taking the crown for themselves? Or at least playing spoiler and wreaking havoc in the National League West?

Seven, five, no, and yes.

Baseball postseason scenarios can be complicated, and it would all boil down to a 10-game tournament to figure out who would have to face a Saint Louis Cardinals who were finishing up their season with a cushioned lead as high as 6 1/2 games over the last week of the season, winning the National League East over the Phillies and allowing the Cardinals the luxury of preparing their team for the upcoming playoffs.

The Braves came out swinging the first two games of their homestand against the San Diego Padres, scoring 23 runs and holding the Padres to 12 to win the first two games easily, before losing the third game as Rick Camp pitched a complete game but gave up the winning run in the ninth inning as Tony Gwynn scored on a Joe Pittman single. The Braves had a golden chance in the bottom of the ninth during the third game with Bob Watson pinch hitting for Camp and drawing a walk. Torre successfully used Brett Butler as a pinch runner with Butler stealing his 21st base of the season. After a strikeout by Claudell Washington, a Rafael Ramirez ground ball moved Butler to third for a chance for Dale Murphy to drive in the run to tie the game. But Murphy grounded out to third base ending the game for a 3–2 San Diego Padres win. The Braves did what was needed, however, by winning two of the three games to pull within one game of the still National West leading Dodgers. Manager Joe Torre understood the importance of each game going forward.

"We did Friday night and today what we have to do the rest of the way," said Torre. "We beat them with the bats, and that is what we got to do the remaining eight games. The bullpen has been our pitching all season, so we've got to outhit them from now on in. Of course, they all are must games now."

But the offense was playing without their recently injured All-Star third baseman, Bob Horner, who had been the thunderous complement to Dale Murphy all season long. "Maybe losing Bob Horner convinced the other players they had to take up the slack. All of them are playing a big part," explained Joe Torre.

Even with all the ups and downs, Torre still believed that the Braves could take the National League West. "Somehow, some way," the Braves would make the postseason. "It's been a little tougher to feel that way lately, but I have," Torre explained. "Despite all the adversity that goes on around here, despite all the streaks and slumps and the injury to Horner. I've always thought we could do it," said Joe Torre as the playoff chase was nearing its end.

The San Francisco Giants continued their late surge as they swept the Dodgers in Los Angeles leaving the Giants tied with the Braves in second place behind the Dodgers.

As the Dodgers kept losing, the Braves and Giants were finding ways to win games down the stretch. The two games for the Braves in San Francisco were a chance to get into first place or fall farther behind. For the long-suffering Torre, who had never appeared in a postseason game as a player or a manager going into his fourth decade, this was a chance to punch his playoff ticket, and the even older Phil Niekro was going to be the player who showed the team how to do it down the stretch.

Niekro took the ball for his 34th start of the season and pitched a complete game shutout for a 7–0 win, giving up only two hits and bringing his win-loss record to a sparkling 16–4 for the season. The Los Angeles Dodgers continued their tailspin, losing their sixth straight game, and the Braves were now tied for first place in the NL West and were aiming to pull ahead of the faltering Dodgers.

The Braves and Dodgers played almost 400 miles apart while they were tied in the standings. By the time the last ball was thrown in their games, one team would be in first place remaining there for the rest of the season.

Rick Mahler took the mound for the Braves in the bottom of the third inning finding himself with a comfortable 6–1 lead after a five-run top of the third inning by the Braves chased Giants starting pitcher Bill Laskey from the game. The Giants were now going to return the favor by knocking Mahler out of the game.

After a flyball out to Joe Morgan, Mahler allowed four runners to reach base via three hits and a walk cutting the lead to 6-3 Braves. Torre pulled the hook removing Mahler from the game in favor of a recently demoted Pascual Perez. It was a leap of faith for Torre as Perez had gone only 1 2/3 innings giving up three earned runs during his last start against the Padres on September 24 and this was his first appearance after being shifted to the bullpen due to his ineffectiveness. In a unique twist, it was Mahler who had to come in relief enroute to an 11-6 Braves victory that day and was replacing Perez in the starting rotation.

Perez rewarded the faith in him as he shutout the Giants for the next 6 2/3 innings and an 8-3 victory. Unexpected players were stepping into key roles for the Braves due to circumstance, and it was paying off as Jerry Royster, Terry Harper, and Pascual Perez pushed the Giants farther back in the race. "Everybody is contributing right now," explained Terry Harper after the win.

Royster was playing for an injured Bob Horner; Terry Harper, who was still in the Braves minor league system as the season started, had 4 RBIs in the 8-3 win and went 6-14 during the two games against the Giants.

The San Francisco Giants were complimentary of the less renown Braves players stepping up in new roles and performing well down the stretch, but the Giants still hoped to rise to the top of the standings themselves.

The Giants were ready to take on the Astros and hoping the Dodgers could keep the Braves from winning more games to allow the Giants to swoop in for the title and beat the Dodgers during the last games of the season. "We're looking up some people," said San Francisco Giants manager Frank Robinson. "Our task is tougher, but it is not over by any means. The best thing that can happen is an L.A. sweep and we have to win a pair from Houston," explained Robinson.

For those who were scoreboard watching, they would have seen the Cincinnati Reds complete a come-from-behind 10th inning 4-3 victory over the Dodgers. The Cincinnati Reds manager was not sure the Los Angeles Dodgers still had the fire it took to finish strong, and the Dodgers manager would have none of that line of thought.

"The way they [the Dodgers] are playing is very surprising to me," Reds manager Russ Nixon explained after the 4–3 Reds victory. "They haven't been doing their work at all. I look across the field and I don't see any spirit. That's unusual for a team that's supposed to be fighting for something. They look like they are dead." But the Dodgers manager Tommy Lasorda tried to exude confidence about his team. "If I didn't have confidence in this team, I'd walk out of this room right now and quit," said Lasorda to reporters in a quiet clubhouse after the loss.

By September 29, the Braves were finally alone atop the National League West again and about to roll into Los Angeles with a chance to put a boot to the Dodgers throat, but even a skidding Dodgers team was a dangerous proposition for the Braves. "We're confident, we're getting more confident, but not overconfident," said Torre about the upcoming games with the Dodgers. And the Atlanta Braves players were not counting the Dodgers out either. "I don't know if you can say the Dodgers are choking, but I hope we can get in and out before they straighten themselves out," explained Braves outfielder Terry Harper on the upcoming games against the Dodgers.

For the Dodgers, their starting pitching was lining up to be far superior to the Braves, with Fernando Valenzuela and Burt Hooton against Tommy Boggs and Rick Camp

The first game was Fernando Valenzuela going for his second attempt at a 20th victory for the season. Tommy Boggs with a 2–2 record for the season seemed on paper like a losing formula for the Braves. But Boggs was once a young pitching sensation, talented enough to be the second overall pick in the 1974 June Amateur Draft by the Texas Rangers out of Lanier High School in Austin, Texas, and he was about to flash those skills keeping the Braves in the game against the great Valenzuela.

The Braves were in a position to put up a run quickly as they had a runner on third base with one out in the top of the first inning, but Valenzuela struck out Dale Murphy, and Bob Watson grounded out to end the threat and keeping it 0-0. Tommy Boggs caused concern in his first inning as he gave up two hits allowing Rick Monday across for Pedro Guerrero's 100th RBI of the season making it 1-0 Dodgers.

Valenzuela finally ran into trouble in the bottom of the fourth as Braves left fielder Terry Harper launched a home run to left field tying the game at 1-1. The Harper home run was just his first home run of the year.

For Harper it had been nearly a decade to that moment after being a 16th round pick by the Braves in the 1973 June Amateur Draft. The 1973 draft had not been too productive for the Braves as only four of the 36 draft picks made it to the MLB level, with Harper having the most successful career over Pat Rockett, Jim Gaudet, and Larry Bradford.

Harper started the year in AAA Richmond tearing up the International League with a .384 across 146 at-bats before being called up and inserted into the lineup on July 2, playing regularly for the Braves for the first time and batting .287 in 150 at-bats after being used sparingly by the Braves in 1980 and 1981.

Jerry Royster followed Harper up with a base hit, eventually scoring on a Glenn Hubbard double putting the Braves ahead 2-1 after the top of the fourth inning.

Tommy Boggs faced 21 batters without allowing a run since the Pedro Guerrero RBI in the first inning, and after Boggs put away Guerrero and Garvey in the bottom of the sixth inning, Torre turned over the game to the Braves bullpen.

For Boggs it was only his 10th start of the year over just 46 1/3 innings pitched and not able to make it through seven innings. It was time to turn it over to rookie sensation Steve Bedrosian who was dominating out the bullpen with 2.42 ERA over 137 2/3 innings pitched, finishing seventh in the National League Rookie of the Year voting.

Bedrosian retired Ron Cey for the third out of the sixth, keeping the Braves lead at 2–1 going into the seventh inning. Fernando Valenzuela pitched a three up and three down seventh inning retiring Chris Chambliss, Rafael Ramirez, and Dale Murphy in order.

Bedrosian stayed in the game allowing Bill Russell a base hit and to eventually score to make it a 2–2 game. The game would remain tied throughout the game until the 12th inning as both teams were able to finally put up runs again.

Ramirez led the top of the 12th inning with a walk and stole second base, and Murphy hit a fly ball for the first out. Bob Watson was intentionally walked filling the vacant first base (replaced by pinch runner Brett Butler) for two chances at a potential inning-ending double play against the upcoming batters of Harper and Royster. But the Braves' chippy youngsters were going to foil the well-thought-out Dodger strategy.

Harper promptly drove Ramirez home, pushing Butler to second base with a base hit to center field and putting the Braves in the lead 3–2, forcing Forster from the game replaced by Dave Stewart.

Royster was about to face his former team for the chance to pile a run on the Braves lead. Royster had made his Major League Baseball debut for the 1973 Dodgers, playing sporadically for the Dodgers until he was traded before the 1976 season to the Braves. Given a chance to play every day, Royster responded by appearing in 149 games and being named to the Topps Rookie All-Star Team at third base.

The former Dodger hit a single to right field driving the speedy Butler in for the run, moving Harper to third base, and moving to second base on the throw. Stewart intentionally walked Hubbard to load the bases for another double play scenario against Matt Sinatro or the light-hitting Garber. Stewart was able to strike out both batters, but the damage had already been done as the Braves were heading to the bottom of the 12th with Garber slated to face a pinch hitter, Dusty Baker, and the MVP candidate Pedro Guerrero.

The pinch-hitting Ken Landreaux singled, bringing up Baker and then Guerrero who had just two hits in 10 at-bats in the game so far. Baker managed a base hit to advance Landreaux to third base. Garber with his side arm delivery was perfect for a double play opportunity. A double play would allow Landreaux to score as the Braves traded the ball from Guerrero to Ramirez for two outs and a 4–3 lead with only one batter to go.

Garvey would be that batter, but the Braves had not been able to get him out all year. Garvey batted a scorching .368 against the 1982 Braves, and after a slow first half batting .252 before the All-Star break, he turned it on, batting a more expected Garvey .313 after the break. But the Braves and Garber would get the best of Garvey in this moment for a fly ball to center field for the 4–3 Braves win and the Dodgers eighth straight loss to drop Los Angeles two games back.

The Braves were now filling up with confidence as there were only four games left for themselves, the San Francisco Giants, and Los Angeles Dodgers. Phil Niekro knew how close the team was to winning a title and he was loving it.

"I don't like to look that far ahead; two games with four to go doesn't mean we have it sewn up," said Niekro. "But it has been satisfying to watch the kids in the organization mature and blend in with the experienced people we traded for. After all the years of losing and suffering, this year has been something special. When you are involved in a pennant race you don't grow old so fast," explained Phil Niekro after the victory.

Jerry Royster saw the game as a way to put even more pressure on the Dodgers. "This puts a lot of pressure on the other two teams, especially the Dodgers," said Royster. "They really needed this game. Now we are on the verge of winning it. We're on a streak. Another win tomorrow night and it is time to close-up shop."

Joe Torre was confident, but not quite as much. "Put it this way, I feel a lot more secure than I did about fours ago," said Torre after the 4–3 Braves victory. "Both teams played their butts off, and I know the feelings the Dodgers have right now. Well, they can't believe what is happening to them. I am glad it is them and not us feeling that right now."

Torre was right about how the Dodgers were feeling in the locker room after the loss. "We've got to win all four games and get some help," said Dodgers manager, Tommy Lasorda. "This is hard to believe." The Dodgers were reeling, and in an unlikely scenario, they hoped the Padres could help them out, but the Dodgers had to first help themselves on September 30 against the Braves.

Burt Hooton took the ball for the Thursday night start in front of nearly 50,000 Dodgers fans in a game feeling like the postseason was coming early. Hooton was a big game pitcher with a World Series resume of winning. Hooton started three games during the 1981 postseason going 3–1 over 25 1/3 innings with a 1.59 ERA, most importantly winning Game 6 on the road of the World Series against the New York Yankees and bringing the trophy back to Los Angeles for the first time since they defeated the Minnesota Twins in 1965.

Rick Camp did not have the experience to match Hooton, and Camp was not pitching especially well going into the game winless in his last five starts. Thankfully for the Braves, they jumped on Hooton for two runs in the first inning with Dale Murphy and Chris Chambliss each knocking in a run making it 2–0 after the top of the first.

The Dodgers clawed back to take the lead with a run in the second and three more in the third as Rick Monday, Steve Sax, and Dusty Baker accounted for a 4–2 Dodgers lead after the bottom of the third inning.

An RBI single by Chambliss driving in Rafael Ramirez and cutting the deficit to 4–3 would be as close as the game would get as the Dodgers piled on more runs in the sixth, seventh, and eighth innings, taking the game 10–3 in a relatively easy win for the Dodgers.

The Braves locker room was not somber and remained upbeat after the loss. "We're not depressed at all," said Joe Torre over loud clubhouse music and banter. "You can see what is going on in here."

After eight straight losses, the Dodgers were on a winning streak of one game toward what they hoped would become four straight games. A return to the playoffs was tantalizingly close for the Dodgers and their fans, but the Giants were finding ways to make sure the road had to go through them first.

As the Dodgers were putting the bow on the 10–3 victory over the Braves, the Giants were running a mad dash to come from behind beating the Astros with seven runs in the final three innings for a walk-off victory.

The Braves were up by one game each to the San Francisco Giants and Los Angeles Dodgers with just three games to go. The good news for the Dodgers was that their bats were awake, rapping out 14 hits during the 10–3 win over the Braves and were about to push the season to the bitter end.

On October 1, the Los Angeles Dodgers were playing the San Francisco Giants on the road, and the Braves were down the coast in San Diego playing, but the three contending teams were in many ways playing each other that night. A loss in San Francisco by either team would end any hope to win the division outright, and a Braves loss in San Diego would open a door allowing for a possible tie in the National League West and an all-or-nothing one-game playoff to decide the division winner.

The Los Angeles Dodgers had another veteran warhorse on the mound going against second-year pitcher Fred Breining for the Giants. The Dodgers Jerry Reuss was a talented pitcher making the All-Star Team twice in his career, placing second in the 1980 National League Award voting to the Philadelphia Phillies Steve Carlton. In fact, a first place vote for Reuss was the only ballot keeping Carlton from receiving a unanimous vote. Reuss also beat Ron Guidry and the Yankees in Game 5 of the 1980 World Series by throwing a 2–1 complete game victory.

In front of 53,281 fans, Reuss was about to toss another big game gem for his 18th victory of the year. Fred Breining battled the Dodgers hard inning after inning, spreading five hits around and not allowing a run. Reuss was matching the zeroes, allowing just one hit all the way as Breining took it to the top of the eighth with a 0-0 score before the Dodgers finally got to him. The top of the eighth started by Breining giving up his fourth walk of the night and putting Steve Sax on base, before striking out Ken Landreaux for the first out. Dusty Baker hit a single and Steve Garvey worked a walk to load the bases for Rick Monday.

For Fred Breining, players in scoring position strangely sharpened his effectiveness. He was able to keep those batters to a paltry .217 batting average compared to a hefty .309 against batters with no runners on for the year, with just one home run against him with a runner in scoring position going into his at-bat with Monday. The veteran Monday had good pop for his career with 242 career home runs, but he hadn't topped the 20-home run plateau since 1976 or hit a Grand Slam since 1973.

The beauty of baseball is it can always happen, and Monday was able to do just that as he launched a home run to center field making the game a 4-0 Dodger lead with his fourth and last Grand Slam of his career. This Grand Slam was the first and only to be allowed by Breining during his career.

The runs on the scoreboard were more than enough as Jerry Reuss continued with his three-hit complete game shutout for a 4-0 victory. Unfortunately for the Dodgers, Phil Niekro and the Braves already had a win in the books that night as Niekro, with just three days' rest, matched the brilliant stat line with a three-hit complete game 4-0 shutout of his own against the San Diego Padres completing his season with a 17-4 win-loss record, a National League best .810 winning percentage. Niekro even put an exclamation mark on his regular season when he hit his seventh career home run helping to win the game.

Although Niekro was cruising along and not allowing a run when he came up in the eighth inning against Eric Show, the game was still very much to be decided as the Braves offense couldn't get runs against the Padres rookie pitcher up to that point. Show pitched a no-hitter until Claudell Washington hit a two-out single scoring Glenn Hubbard and making it a 1-0 Braves lead.

Joe Torre displayed a mammoth amount of trust by keeping Niekro in the game to bat with Hubbard in scoring position at second base with one out, after catcher Bruce Benedict moved Hubbard over with a sacrifice bunt to first base for Niekro to have the chance to bring a run in. Most managers in that spot would have put in a pinch hitter, but Torre was going to roll the dice and see it pay off as Niekro took Snow's pitch and deposited it into the stands for his first home run since 1976 making it a 3-0 Braves lead.

After the game Niekro and Torre talked about the at-bat. "I don't think I was so surprised that I hit the ball hard," said Niekro. "I was more surprised that I hit in that situation." From Torre's point of view, it seemed like he was willing to concede the second out by Niekro and keep him in the game to pitch the ninth inning. "I'd be a liar if I said I was bunting him [Hubbard] over for Knucksie," Torre said. "I was bunting him over for Claudell [Washington], hoping we could get one more run. Hopefully we can get some more of these surprises in the next few days," explained Torre after Niekro hit his first home run of the season.

Niekro saved his best pitching of the year for when the Braves needed it most, closing out his season with 24 consecutive shutout innings and allowing just 10 hits over his last three starts. He was amped up between his two shutouts and his comments from the night before his second shutout reveal his enthusiasm for the stretch run. "All I can say is that I have been geared up for this week for 13 years. This is what I have been waiting for," explained Niekro on the big game atmosphere.

One of the other Braves was no stranger to playing huge October games. For him, the team aspect was everything, and there was also a personal goal he wanted badly.

On October 14, 1976, Chris Chambliss launched a game-winning bottom of the ninth home run propelling the New York Yankees over the Kansas City Royals for their first American League Pennant in 12 years and the first of three straight trips to the World Series. Chambliss knew big home runs, but for him, a 20th home run in a season was still not on his playing resume.

Chambliss was the kind of player personified by the term "professional hitter," but he was not the power hitting stereotype like his contemporaries Willie Stargell, Steve Garvey, Eddie Murray, and George Scott. More than 40 years later, in 2025, Chambliss, reflected on having hit the 20-home run plateau in both 1982 and 1983:

> I was able to put up solid home run numbers, hitting double digits sometimes, getting up to 17 a couple of time or so with the Yankees and was up to 18 with the Braves, but I wasn't a big power hitter like a lot of first baseman, but I was still able to drive in a lot of runs.... Being able to get to 20 home runs was a signal that I did have some power, I was glad to be able to hit that mark a couple of times with the Braves,

It was even better for Chambliss that his 20th home run of 1982 was able to help put game 161 away for the Braves.

By the time the Braves were squaring off in San Diego against the Padres on the night of October 2, the Dodgers had already crushed the San Francisco Giants 15–2 earlier that day up the coast in San Francisco. The Braves had to win their game to keep sole possession of first place in the National League West. Wrong Way Pascual Perez, starting the game, was going to have to point the way for the Braves.

Perez was making his first start after being replaced in the starting rotation a couple of weeks before, but he had pitched effectively in two appearances out of the Braves bullpen allowing 0 earned runs in 7 2/3 innings.

The Braves scoring began with a Glenn Hubbard base hit scoring Terry Harper and making it a 1–0 Braves lead in the top of the second inning. The Braves added a Rafael Ramirez sacrifice fly to make it 2–0 during the top of the third.

After Dale Murphy was called out at third base attempting to stretch a double into a triple, Chris Chambliss batted against John Montefusco and deposited the pitch into the right field stands for his 20th home run, putting the Braves in front 3-0 after the top of the third. The home run was the difference in the game as the Braves were able to hold the Padres to a run in the bottom of the fourth and one more in the bottom of the sixth. The Braves added an insurance run in the top of the ninth with a Bob Watson pinch hit RBI to left field scoring Jerry Royster for a 4-2 lead.

Gene Garber took the mound for the Braves for the bottom of the ninth, closing the door against the Padres for his 30th save of the year and the Braves 89th win and keeping the Dodgers a game back in the standings with just one game to play.

The Dodgers victory on Saturday eliminated the Giants from the championship, but would the Giants just roll over on the Sunday and not give the Dodgers their best effort? The answer to anyone who knew the Giants' manager, Frank Robinson, was an easy one, and the Dodgers were about to find out, as the Giants were going to fight hard to return the favor of their season being ended by the Dodgers.

Major League Baseball was going to end the 1982 season with pure excitement with two division crowns on the line as the Milwaukee Brewers were also playing the Baltimore Orioles tied in the American League East. Whichever team could win their 95th game would play the American League West champion Los Angeles Dodgers for the chance to play in the World Series.

The Atlanta Braves and Milwaukee Brewers were playing Sunday October 3 for the chance to keep the dream of an Atlanta Braves versus Milwaukee Brewers World Series, but first the teams needed to win. The thought may have excited the fans of those cities, but for the players there was a game to be won and a League Championship to get through.

The Braves would be going against the Padres and their top pitcher Tim Lollar, who was having his breakout in his third year going for his 16th win of the season and a chance for the San Diego Padres to finish their season at .500 for the first time since 1978 (84-78); this would be only the second time in their franchise history to finish at .500 or better. The Padres were on an upward trajectory, and the game outcome mattered to them.

The Braves could not roll out Phil Niekro again after he tossed a shutout a couple of days before, nor could they use the dynamic youngster Pascual Perez who pitched the previous night, so the choice for Joe Torre was reliever-turned-starting pitcher, Rick Camp on short rest. His last start had only been four innings in a 10-3 loss to the Dodgers on September 30. The hope was that he could replicate the pitching performance of his September 26 start against the Padres when he threw a complete game only allowing two runs in a 3-2 loss. The Braves would just need to score some runs.

The San Diego Padres and Atlanta Braves bobbed and weaved with Lollar and Camp exchanging zeroes until the Atlanta Braves finally broke through for their first hit of the game against Lollar during the top of the fifth inning, when Terry Harper sent a ball into the left field stands for his second home run of the year and putting the Braves in front for a 1-0 lead.

Harper hitting a home run was not something seen often for the 1982 Braves. He had finally hit his first home run of his season the week before when he took Fernando Valenzuela deep over the left field wall in the fourth inning tying the game 1-1 during the eventual 4-3 Braves victory over the Los Angeles Dodgers. Harper had his first home run in 133 at-bats, and it would only take 16 more at-bats for him to find the seats again. The left fielder was stepping into a vacant power vacuum left by the Braves' two best home run hitters.

The power bats of Dale Murphy and Bob Horner were absent down the stretch run with Murphy hitting just two home runs in 63 at-bats, and Horner missing games the previous two weeks due to injury and stroking only two home runs in his final 27 at-bats. But the Harper home run did not supply the spark for the Braves offense as Lollar shut down the side in order after the

Harper blast. The Braves' Camp was going to have to hold the Padres for a chance to win.

Camp was pitching a gem, allowing only two hits, no walks, and no runs clinging to a 1-0 lead going into the bottom of the fifth against the Padres. At approximately the same time, Valenzuela and the Dodgers were knotted up with the Giants at 2-2. This would be the last time the Braves would be out in front controlling their playoff destiny as they would need to rely on one division rival to beat another division rival.

Camp began the bottom of the fifth by giving up a base hit to the rookie Tony Gwynn. Camp allowed the first four batters to get on base tying the game at 1-1. With the bases loaded, the speedy rookie center fielder Alan Wiggins hit a base-clearing triple putting the San Diego Padres up 4-1.

The Braves were forced to use the bullpen, replacing Camp with Donnie Moore to try to stop the bleeding. Moore came in to get the next three outs only allowing a sacrifice fly scoring Wiggins from third and bringing the Padres to a commanding 5-1 lead.

The Braves were done with their offense for the day not scoring again as Luis DeLeon and Dave Dravecky took the game over for Lollar and the Padres in the sixth inning, shutting the Braves down the rest of the way for a 5-1 win, bringing the Padres their second .500 or better record in their franchise history.

The San Diego Padres with their exciting nucleus of players were on their way to four straight .500 or better seasons including a thrilling 1984 National League Championship win over the Chicago Cubs winning after being down two games in the five-game NLCS, and their first World Series appearance losing to the Detroit Tigers in five games.

By 1984, the Padres built their winning team in a manner similar to what the Braves and Ted Turner were trying to do, as the Padres combined older, big-name free agents with an emerging home-grown core.

This strategy would work for the Padres as first baseman Steve Garvey, third baseman Graig Nettles, and closer Goose Gossage were able to remain relatively injury free, blending with Garry Templeton, Terry Kennedy, Kevin McReynolds, Alan Wiggins, and Tony Gwynn to make their World Series appearance and four straight .500 or better seasons.

Just as the Braves' Matt Sinatro made the last out of the Braves game, ensuring an 89-win regular season for the Braves, the Dodgers were still tied at 2–2 in the top of the seventh at Candlestick. As the game progressed, the fans, players, and everyone knew the Dodgers had a chance to push the season to a one-game playoff with the Atlanta Braves to decide the National League West title and the right to play the Saint Louis Cardinals.

The Braves' Ted Turner, Joe Torre, players, coaches, and staff were all huddling around one small color television broadcasting their playoff fate. It would be an agonizing 45 minutes with each pitch, play, and out met with anticipation.

For the Dodgers' Fernando Valenzuela, this would be his third attempt to win his 20th game of the 1982 season, but the only thing that mattered to him and the team in that moment was a win to tie the Braves with 89 wins. Valenzuela pitched well, just allowing two runs through six innings before giving the ball to a usually excellent Tom Niedenfuer out of the Dodgers bullpen.

The seventh inning began a flurry of moves from the bench from both the Dodgers and Giants as the last three innings could end the Dodgers season. A total of 15 roster substitutions occurred in the last three innings as Tommy Lasorda and Frank Robinson swapped pitchers, runners, and batters, attempting to put the game away with 10 roster moves in the fateful seventh inning.

Right-handed pitcher Tom Niedenfuer replaced Jorge Orta in the bottom of the seventh Dodgers lineup; Orta had earlier replaced Valenzuela as a pinch hitter during the top the seventh. Niedenfuer gave a leadoff single to Bob Brenly, and the pinch-hitting Champ Summers promptly doubled to left field in his at-bat for Joe Pettini. Summers gave way to pinch runner Guy Sularz at second base, as Brenly was at third base. Lasorda kept Niedenfuer to face Greg Minton, the Giants pitcher. Niedenfuer struck out Minton for the first out. Lasorda strolled out to take the ball from Niedenfuer who was angry at being pulled from the game as Lasorda called for the left-handed Terry Forster from the Dodgers bullpen as the Giants had Jim Wohlford to pinch-hit for Max Venable.

The Dodgers were one out from ending the Giants threat after Forster struck out Jim Wohlford, but Joe Morgan was about to step to the plate for another brilliant moment of his Hall of Fame career.

Although Morgan was far removed from his Big Red Machine MVP winning days, he was still a good hitter batting .289, OPS+ of 136, and an All-Star level of 5.1 WAR. Morgan could still bring it at 38 years old and was about to bring the Braves in the Padres visiting clubhouse to elation.

Morgan launched a Terry Forster pitch into the right field stands for a home run, driving in three runs and putting the Giants in front of the Dodgers 5–2. Giants' pitcher Greg Minton remained in the game giving up back-to-back doubles with Ken Landreaux and Dusty Baker closing the lead to 5–3 for the Giants with just one out in the inning, but Minton responded by retiring Garvey and Monday to end the Dodgers eighth-inning threat.

Forster did his job by retiring the Giants in order during the bottom of the eighth to keep the game within striking distance for the Dodgers.

The game was going to the top of the ninth with Minton still on the mound facing Ron Cey, Ron Roenicke, and Bill Russell—with Minton winning all three at-bats and retiring the Dodgers in order, finally delivering the National League West to the Braves and sending them to the postseason for the first time since 1969.

Greg Minton took a special pride in taking down their division foe, the World Champion Dodgers:

I have nothing personal against anyone on the Dodgers, but when we realized they could be in it if they won, our whole bench got keyed up. I was more pumped than I'd been in three years, and did you see that reaction after Joe's homer? It's a special feeling to see them not get in because of us. After all they're the Dodgers,

The Braves' next opponent, the Saint Louis Cardinals, had some players who were pleased to see the Dodgers out of the playoffs as well. "It was getting stale with the Dodgers around every year," said Cardinal Dane Iorg. "It was time for some new blood. I'm tired of all that hugging and kissing they do.... I'm happy for the Braves and I'm glad to see other clubs share the spotlight."

In San Diego it was pure joy and pandemonium in the visitor's club house as the Braves watched Ron Cey make the third out of the inning bringing the Braves to the National League West title.

Perhaps the strangest sight to see in the joyous Braves locker room was the San Diego Chicken being asked, "Why did the chicken cross the road," with the San Diego Chicken audibly declaring, "To take the Braves to the playoffs," while drinking champagne straight from the bottle next to Ted Turner and Braves' announcer Skip Caray.

In perhaps one of the most bizarre Ted Turner efforts to entertain Braves fans, he had proposed a trade to the San Diego Padres at the 1978 owners' meetings that would have sent the Padres a player for the Chicken. However, the Chicken was not a team asset and was employed by a local San Diego radio station. Ted Turner would not be deterred so easily. Later in 1978, Turner offered the person who played the Chicken, Ted Giannoulas, $100,000 scribbled on the back of a business card, to leave KGB Radio and work for Turner. Giannoulas was not swayed and stayed cooped up in San Diego, continuing his mascot career for decades. A San Diego Chicken costume is displayed at the National Baseball Hall of Fame.

Whatever road the Chicken crossed to help the Braves to the playoffs was not an easy road to cross as the 1982 season could only be described as a topsy-turvy roller coaster of a season with the Braves' fate undetermined until well after their last out.

Manager Joe Torre knew just how crazy a season it was and couldn't help but find the romantic side of baseball within it. "We've been at death's door a couple of times this year, but no one could close us out. I am so proud of this team. It has been so resilient," said Joe Torre. "It's been nice to watch us pull together and refuse to be torn apart. It sounds kind of romantic, doesn't it? And in my mind, it is romantic," explained Torre during the celebration in the locker room.

And for superstar Dale Murphy, it didn't matter how they won it, they did it. "I don't care how we did it, it is done. We've just taken the longest and toughest step," explained Murphy.

But the toughest step was still on the horizon in the form of the Saint Louis Cardinals.

7

The 1982 Playoffs

A huge obstacle for the Braves was forming on the horizon in the form of rain, and this was about to muddy the Braves' efforts to go to the World Series.

The World Series would in some ways be a homecoming for Joe Torre and Braves coaches Bob Gibson (Hall of Fame pitcher) and Dal Maxvill.

Torre won the National League MVP Award as a player for the Cardinals in 1971, and Gibson earned the National League Cy Young Award and the National League MVP Award in his 1968 season, which was one of the finest seasons in the history of Major League Baseball.

Gibson—with his 1.12 ERA across 304 2/3 innings with 268 strikeouts and holding batters to a measly .184 batting average—was one of the reasons why the pitching mounds were lowered from 15 inches to 10 inches in 1969, to give batters more of a chance against pitchers. The year 1968 was indeed the "year of the pitcher," with amazing feats in pitching. The Tigers' Denny McLain won 31 games. Don Drysdale of the Dodgers set a record with 58 2/3 consecutive scoreless innings pitched. But Gibson's performance even surpassed the dominance of McLain and Drysdale, as Gibson's 1.12 earned run average (ERA) was the lowest of any pitcher since the Deadball Era decades before. Gibson threw 28 complete games, including 13 shutouts, to unanimously win the National League Cy Young Award. Even with a lower pitching mound and a tightened strike zone beginning in 1969, Gibson still won 20 or more games in the 1969 and 1970 seasons winning the 1970 National League Cy Young Award.

The notoriously competitive Gibson had only one allegiance, however, as the Braves were getting ready to square off against his former team in 1982. "There is no emotion for me playing the Cardinals; I just want to beat the bleep out of them, that's all. I go where my paycheck is. That's who my loyalty is with," said Gibson.

For Dal Maxvill, the former long-time Cardinals infielder who played in three World Series for the team, his response was a little more tempered. "Because of my career in St. Louis, I prefer to look at it like I'm trying to help the Braves win, rather than stop the Cardinals from winning," Maxvill explained.

Joe Torre summed it up succinctly: "Obviously, I like the way the Cardinals do things, because I hired two Cardinals as my coaches. All three of us have soft spots for Saint Louis, but we won't feel them this week."

Torre was right, all three did have soft spots for the Cardinals, with all three returning to that organization at some point over the years: Maxvill went back to Saint Louis as their general manager from 1985 to 1994, bringing the team to World Series appearances in 1985 and 1987. Torre returned to the team as manager from 1990 until he was replaced early in the season in 1995. Torre was even able to bring Gibson back to the Cardinals in 1995 as pitching coach, and Torre also brought in former Braves with Chris Chambliss as a hitting coach in 1995.

For 1982, it was purely an allegiance to the Braves and beating Saint Louis as Phil Niekro and his ageless arm were poised to topple the Cardinals, but Niekro would run out of time.

There were three people in uniform for the Braves on Wednesday, October 6, 1982, who had also been in uniform for the Braves the previous time the team was in postseason play. Coaches Tommie Aaron and Sonny Jackson, who at 42 and 37 years old, respectively, were younger than the 43-year-old Niekro. Two other Braves coaches in 1982 had also been in uniform in the 1969 National League Championship Series, as Joe Pignatano was the Mets bullpen coach, and Rube Walker was the Mets pitching coach.

The record books do not show the 1982 National League Championship in its full context. The records show the Cardinals sweeping the Braves 3-0 by a 17-5 score with 34 hits to the Braves 15, batting .330 and holding the Braves to a .169 batting average. All of this is true, but it could have been very different with the Braves jumping up 1-0 behind Niekro pitching his third straight shutout. We don't see this because the official record is washed away by rain and replaced by a Saint Louis Cardinals 7-0 shutout the next day.

In the Wednesday afternoon opener, the Braves jumped out to a 1-0 lead with Claudell Washington hitting a triple and Chambliss driving him in to put the Braves on top for a first-inning lead.

Phil Niekro started out the game with the 1-0 lead in steady, hard rain, and he was able to keep the Cardinals from doing much as he shut down Saint Louis 1-0 going into the bottom of the fifth inning, just three batters away from an official game, with the rain not showing any chance of stopping.

With a quick victory on Wednesday, Niekro (who would be able to start two games in a five-game series) would potentially be available in an "All-Hands on Deck" scenario out of the bullpen on an abbreviated basis as the NLCS went on. This could have put the Braves in a stronger position as Niekro was the best pitcher in baseball coming into the postseason.

As Niekro gathered his first out in the bottom of the fifth, home plate umpire Billy Williams knew he was going to be up against it no matter what he did. If the game went official, the Saint Louis home crowd would boo and go nuts if he had to call the game later with the Braves still in front, or let the game keep going under conditions that Williams felt could not be played to nine innings. So with pitcher Joaquin Andujar digging into the batter's box, Williams stopped the game for a rain delay at 3:44 that afternoon.

All Niekro wanted was the chance to finish the inning to make it an official game in case the rain would not stop. "I was disappointed, I think any pitcher would have been disappointed, whether it is a playoff situation or a regular season game," said Niekro. With the window quickly closing on any chance for the game, he knew each pitch was bringing him closer to a lead in the playoffs.

Cardinals manager Whitey Herzog also knew each second of rain could bring the game to a rain delay, and he wanted the delay before the game could become official. Perhaps Herzog was sly like a fox as he deployed game-stalling tactics while the rain came pouring down, flooding the Astro Turf, and making game play less likely with each pitch.

The stalls in the game were as thick as the rain with Herzog arguing repeatedly that Niekro was balking with his pitches. Each visit to the umpire was precious time taken from Niekro and the Braves, who were trying to push the game to an official status. "Whitey came to me and argued about balks twice during the game," said Billy Williams. "I discussed Niekro's move with my colleagues on the field during the game and after it was halted. We feel his stop was good enough. As long as there is a pause, a hesitation, it's not a balk," explained Williams on the Whitey Herzog arguments. Herzog disagreed with Williams and his interpretation of the balk rule. "I think Niekro balked about 7 or 8 times," said Herzog. "Rule 805, paragraph M, says when a pitcher throws from a set position, he has to come to complete stop."

The arguments of "Pause," "Hesitation," and "Stop" between the umpires and Herzog took time away from Niekro to get his outs and to let it continue raining.

After the game, Niekro would not admit to balking. "All I can say is I've been pitching in the Big Leagues 19 years and haven't changed my style," he explained. "Maybe I could have done it with two or three pitches, or maybe 10–15. I was just upset I didn't have the chance to get two more batters out."

Atlanta Brave manager Torre seemed to balance his annoyance with empathy for the position Williams and the umpires were in. "I was told the same rules apply for the playoffs; during the regular season the umpires try to get five innings in," said Torre. But he then gave a nod to the reality of the situation. "If the game had been called after five innings there would have been a lot of heat on the umpires," Torre explained.

Torre seems to have a different recollection of the rain picking up as the first out in the bottom of the fifth was made forcing the rain delay. "It was raining, but not raining hard at the time Billy called it. I am not bitter, but I think we should have been given the opportunity to get the outs," said Joe Torre. "There is no animosity on my part," Torre further noted.

The umpire claimed the game would have been put in rain delay regardless of the stature of the game. "I would have stopped it when I did whether it was a regular season game or a playoff," Williams said, disagreeing with Joe Torre. "The rain became heavier after the first out."

But Williams then said something blowing up his own words and backing up Torre's argument that an umpire would have let the game play through five innings to at least make it an official game going into a rain delay during the regular season. "I didn't want anyone criticized, whether the National League executives or the umpiring crew, that we played through a downpour just to get the last two outs and call it," said Williams. "Stopping it when I did was fair for both sides."

Whether or not the umpiring crew changed the way the game was called from the regular season, it certainly did the Saint Louis Cardinals a big favor, and Saint Louis manager Whitey Herzog knew how big a break this was. "We were lucky, it was a break for us. We were down a run and got past their best pitcher, it favors us because Niekro can start just once more," explained Herzog after the game was rained out and giving the Saint Louis Cardinals a do-over for game one and not having to face Niekro in it.

The real game one was now on Thursday night in Saint Louis. The veteran pitcher Bob Forsch of the Cardinals versus the Braves youngster, Pascual Perez, with Billy Williams as the home plate umpire again, but this time under dry skies with 53,008 fans in attendance.

Forsch was a steady to good pitcher for the Saint Louis Cardinals from 1974 to 1988, before finishing his career in 1988–1989 with the Houston Astros with a 168–136 win-loss record highlighted with a 20-win 1977 season, and two Silver Slugger Awards recognizing him as the NL best-hitting pitcher.

For both pitchers it would be their first taste of postseason on the mound—and they both came out slinging. Forsch retired the first six Braves batters in order, with Perez returning the favor against the Cardinals.

The Braves finally were able to get a runner on base against Forsch during the top of the third as Bruce Benedict was able to reach base on an error with one out after a Glenn Hubbard strike out. Perez was unable to move Benedict over to second base as he fouled off a two-strike bunt attempt for the second out. But the Braves were still showing life with two outs as Claudell Washington hit a single to center field and catcher Benedict advanced from first to third base with the hit.

The good bat of Rafael Ramirez had the chance to give the Braves an early lead in the game as he dug in for his at-bat against Forsch. The young Dominican shortstop was a slick fielder, still prone to making errors in the field, but he was able to cover up his blemishes by bringing a live bat and speed to the Braves lineup. That was especially true as Ramirez hit .297 during the second half of the 1982 season, after hitting just .259 for the first half. Ramirez was really coming on offensively for the Braves postseason push as he batted .324 with a powerful .865 OPS for September and October, with five home runs and 19 RBIs. For comparison, Dale Murphy batted .230 with a .799 OPS during the same time frame with four home runs and 12 RBIs.

Ramirez, with Murphy right behind him in the batting order as protection, was having good opportunities to help the Braves win games. But the scenario of a runner on first and third with two outs was not a situation that Ramirez was able to deliver on well during the regular season as he had just three hits in 13 at-bats, driving in three runs for a .231 batting average, with a .517 OPS. Unfortunately for Ramirez and the Braves, he hit a groundball to shortstop for a force at second base to end the threat and leave two men on base. It would be as close as the Braves would get as they were only able to get two more runners on base for the entire game.

For the Cardinals, it would take them just their next two batters to bring them all the runs needed to win the game. The 23-year-old speedster rookie, Willie McGee, led off the bottom of the third inning with a triple against Perez to set up a sacrifice fly by the next batter, Ozzie Smith, to give the Saint Louis Cardinals a 1–0 lead.

Perez was able to keep the game at a 1–0 Cardinals lead going into the top of the sixth inning. Up to that point the game was a pitching duel between Forsch and Perez, but the bottom of the sixth inning started off disastrously for Perez. Lonnie Smith, Keith Hernandez, and George Hendrick hit consecutive singles against Perez to lead off the top of the sixth, making it a 2–0 Cardinals lead and knocking Perez out of the game for relief specialist Steve Bedrosian.

The often spectacular Bedrosian did not show his best stuff that day. He was unable to stop the Braves bleeding by allowing a walk, three singles, and a sacrifice fly, and throwing a wild pitch while recording just two outs to eight batters before turning the ball over to Donnie Moore. After hitting Smith with a pitch, Moore was able to retire Hernandez, batting for his second time in the inning, and who hit a flyball for the third out. By the end of this "death by six singles," the Braves were down 6–0.

This would be more than enough for Forsch on the mound as he retired the next nine Braves batters in order, allowing just one ball past the infield during his last three innings pitched to shut down the Braves 7–0.

Over 42 years after the Game One loss, a decision made still rolls around the brain of Joe Torre. "I don't know, with how it all worked out, maybe I should have given Phil Niekro the chance to go back out there in the other game one," said Torre. "Who knows."

But back in 1982, the Braves and Torre went with the young and talented Perez, gambling on a close game and victory, and perhaps giving the ball to Niekro the next night on game two for a good chance at a commanding 2–0 game lead and closing the series with the sweep in Atlanta. That was a good script to go for anyways.

Torre was still up in the air about turning the ball over to Niekro for game two on short rest the next night, and Niekro was lobbying hard for the ball. As a catcher, Torre had caught thousands of Niekro knuckle balls and batted against hundreds of the wobblers from Phil and Joe Niekro over the years, and Torre was prepared to gamble by naming Tommy Boggs as the Game Two starter.

To have Boggs named as the starter was frustrating for Phil, as he had even lobbied Torre to pitch the day after his rained-out Game One's 4 1/3 innings pitched. The tireless Niekro wanted the ball badly for the Friday night game after the Game One 7–0 loss. He tried to put on a brave face after Torre announced that Boggs would be the Game Two starting pitcher that Friday night. "You're always excited about pitching and disappointed when you don't," explained Niekro after learning he was scheduled for Game Three by Torre. But the rain had taken away a National League Championship Series pitching start on Wednesday night, and the rain was now going to ensure Niekro would get the chance for a Game Two start.

After a downpour on Friday rained out the Braves and Cardinals game for a second time in three days, it looked like there could be a break for the Braves. Niekro could now pitch game two, and perhaps also be available later in the series if needed in game five.

But for the Braves' scheduled game two pitcher Boggs, the night of the second rainout was a bitter pill to take. "That's great, but we didn't win a 162-game season with one pitcher," said Boggs, the young pitcher after the game was canceled. "I was psyched to pitch. We thought they would stay all night to get this one in," he explained.

For Phil Niekro, it was a chance to step into his role as the anchor of the rotation, and perhaps he could soothe some hurt feelings between himself and Joe Torre. "I was ready to pitch tonight [Friday]. I'll be ready to pitch tomorrow [Saturday]," said Niekro after the game two rainout. But perhaps the extra time allowed Niekro to understand why Torre planned to schedule Boggs in the first place.

"If I was in his position, I might have done the same thing," offered Niekro, referring to Torre's original revised plans. But Niekro was still quick to point out that he wanted the start in the first place. "At the same time, he [Torre] knew that I was concerned because I was ready."

"If anybody's disappointed, it's probably Tommy Boggs. He was ready to pitch tonight. It is something over which we have no control," said Niekro after the Friday night washout.

Boggs did not get into the 1982 NLCS, or any other playoff game in his career; he never even made another major league pitching start. Boggs appeared in five games out of the Braves bullpen in 1983 and was released by the club in October after dealing with a rotator cuff injury in the 1982–1983 seasons. Boggs worked his way back with the Rangers in 1985, appearing in four games as a reliever. The second-overall pick of the 1974 MLB draft retired at 29 years old after his 1985 season, eventually becoming the head baseball coach at Concordia University Texas in 2009, winning 325 games over 13 seasons before his death in 2022 at the age of 66.

Days after Phil Niekro's 4 1/3 rainout on the Wednesday night, he was going to get the ball with a chance to even the series up 1–1, and hopefully go home to Atlanta and win two of the next three games at Atlanta-Fulton County Stadium.

John Stuper, a 25-year-old rookie, would take the mound for the Cardinals on Saturday night. Stuper was having a strong season as a starter, slotting in behind Joaquín Andujar and Bob Forsch, going 9–7 with a respectable 3.36 ERA in 136 2/3 innings pitched. Stuper finished his season strong as he pitched to a 2.74 ERA over August and October, in his 82 IP going into the playoffs.

Stuper quickly set a tone for the game as he put Claudell Washington away with a fly ball and struck out the next two batters to retire the Braves in order during the top of the first inning. After having shut out all of baseball over the last couple of weeks, Phil Niekro was about to have a more difficult time.

The leadoff hitter, Tommy Herr, was able to draw a five-pitch walk from Niekro, putting the pitcher on his heels quickly during the bottom of the first. Ken Oberkfell did the Braves a favor by hitting a groundball and wiping out the speedy Herr with a force out at second base. A base hit by Smith pushed Oberkfell to third base, making it first and third with only one out. Keith Hernandez, a smart hitter who typically would be able to find a way to bring the run in from third with one out, grounded out for a second out. The next batter Darrell Porter was able to take first base with wild pitch ball four that scored Oberkfell from third base. George Hendrick hit into the third groundout of the inning. The Cardinals with a death by a thousand cuts to the Braves sent six batters to the plate and with only one hit, two walks, and a wild pitch enabled the scrappy Whitey Herzog team an early 1-0 lead against the previously unscathed Niekro and the Braves.

Niekro and Stuper traded scoreless frames in the second inning, before Niekro helped his own offense in the third inning.

Bruce Benedict batting out of the eighth spot walked leading off the top of the first inning. Niekro as a veteran pitcher could handle his bat well enough to occasionally have a base hit and lay down a sacrifice to help his team. He put down a sacrifice bunt that was good enough to get Benedict over to second base with just one out. Washington was not able to bring Benedict home, however, as he struck out looking for the second out. The hot hitting Rafael Ramirez then delivered a single to centerfield bringing home Benedict, and Ramirez was able to make it all the way around to home on an error to make the score 2-1, officially the first lead for the Braves in the NLCS at the top of the third inning. It really all could come together for the Braves as their ace Niekro was on the mound looking to get the win before going home to Atlanta.

Phil Niekro and John Stuper both pitched well with no scoring until the top of the fifth inning when Niekro was about to inflict some damage on Stuper.

Going into the top of the fifth, Stuper only allowed two base hits all game, but the first two batters were able to tag him with a single and a ground-rule double, bringing up Niekro with runners on second and third with no outs. This was a situation that Niekro had faced just once in 1982. The only other situation with second and third with no outs resulted in a Niekro strike-out.

A sacrifice fly to score the runner from third is not a sure outcome for any professional baseball hitter, and for a pitcher it is even more difficult. During Niekro's long career, he only hit 12 sacrifice fly balls. But Niekro took the first pitch from Stuper and was able to push the ball deep enough in outfield air to bring home Glenn Hubbard for a 3-1 lead in the fifth inning. Niekro now had a hand in two of the three runs the Braves were able to put across the plate.

The game remained a 3-1 Braves lead until Darrell Porter drove in Keith Hernandez with a double to right field tightening the game to a 3-2 Braves lead. The four-hit, four-walk, one-run sixth inning would be the last inning in the game for Niekro, bringing his pitching stat line for the night to six innings, six hits, and two earned runs while throwing 97 pitches. It was not quite the game the Braves or Niekro himself had seen during his last few starts, but he did his job, handing the ball over to the Braves bullpen as he hoped to pitch later in the series.

Stuper was also done with his sixth inning; he pitched as well as Niekro, keeping the Cardinals close enough to win by allowing just four base hits, two earned runs, and one walk in his six innings pitched, only throwing 78 pitches.

Doug Bair came in from the Cardinals bullpen for the top of the seventh and gave the Braves a golden chance to further their lead by allowing Jerry Royster to lead off the inning with a single. Bair walked a tightrope by navigating the Braves lineup with a sacrifice bunt for an out, a walk, a groundout, and an intentional walk to load the bases with two outs with Rafael Ramirez coming up. Issuing the intentional pass to Claudell Washington to get to Ramirez worked as Ramirez hit a flyball ending the inning and the Braves' bases loaded threat.

Gene Garber came in for Niekro, looking like he was indeed one of baseball's best relievers and a formidable Braves rebuttal for the Cardinals "All-Everything" closer, Bruce Sutter. Garber struck out two in the seventh and retired Ken Oberkfell with a groundout for three outs.

Whitey Herzog was sticking with Bair to start the bottom of the eighth inning. Dale Murphy came through with his first base hit of the NLCS, and promptly stole second base on the second pitch to the next batter Chris Chambliss. The Cardinals then opted to issue an intentional walk to Chambliss setting up an at-bat between Bob Horner and the incoming Bruce Sutter, who was relieving Bair. With a slow runner now on first and one in the box with Horner, a groundball would be an easy two outs, and a pitcher like Sutter was one of the best at keeping the ball down in the zone.

Sutter faced five batters with men on first and second bases with no outs during the 1982 season, each time not allowing the batter to get on base or bring in a run. A big reason for Sutter's success was his ability to throw a split-finger fastball. It was a pitch that took Sutter from a fringe pitching prospect all the way to the Baseball Hall of Fame.

Sutter was able to master the pitch with his exceptionally long fingers and good wrist control and bringing incredible down spin to the ball, creating a pitch that looks like a strike suddenly diving down at the last nanosecond before it reaches the plate and leaving the batter flailing at the ball in disbelief. Sutter was able to lead the National League in 1982 with 36 saves with the pitch as his bread and butter. A flip side of the pitch could be that it was difficult to handle for a catcher hoping to throw out a base runner. But the Cardinals pulled it off beautifully against the Braves.

Horner struck out on a 2–2 pitch leaving runners on first and second with one out. Murphy tried to steal third base on the first pitch to Jerry Royster during the next at-bat, hoping to set up the Braves with a sacrifice fly scenario, but it backfired as Porter nailed Murphy at third base during the attempt and the second out. Royster, with two outs and Chambliss at first base, would end the threat by hitting into a groundout and ending the inning. Sutter evaded the Braves, keeping the game to a tight 3-2 Braves lead going into the bottom of the eighth inning.

The Cardinals executed "Whitey Ball" to perfection against Gene Garber during the eighth to generate a run to tie the game. After a groundout by the leadoff batter, Porter worked a walk, and the catcher was able to hustle first to third on a Hendrick single to center field to set the table for Willie McGee with a runner on first and third with just one out.

McGee was able to muster a ground ball to the shortstop who could only get a force-out at second base with the blazing McGee scorching to first as Porter scored the tying run knotting it at 3-3. Ozzie Smith ended the inning with a groundout, but finally the game was tied and they were going into the ninth.

Bruce Sutter continued his dominance by setting the Braves down in order during the top of the ninth to allow the Cardinals to try to walk it off for the win against Gene Garber and the Braves.

David Green, who had replaced Lonnie Smith the previous inning, led off with a single. Playing small ball, Tommy Herr was able to put down a sacrifice bunt moving Green into scoring position. The Cardinals would now be likely to win with a base hit by one of the next two batters. Oberkfell took his second pitch, just a little in on the plate, from Garber and hit it into right-center field just past the glove of rookie Brett Butler for the base hit, scoring Green from second base for the 4-3 walk-off victory, and the commanding 2-0 lead in the NLCS going into Atlanta.

The Braves now had their backs against the wall and needed to win the next three games. After the game Joe Torre had plenty of second guessing on some of his decisions but seemed to have sound rationale behind all of them. There was just one decision that would seem to have generated some further bad feelings.

Why even pitch to Oberkfell with Sutter following him? With Hernandez following Sutter in the batting order, pitching to Oberkfell was a more palatable choice than facing the more formidable Hernandez in the huge spot. "I was looking at Oberkfell or Hernandez. It was like being between a rock and a hard place. As far as walking Oberkfell to get Sutter out of the game, I wasn't even thinking about that because if we can't get out the jam, there isn't a game and it doesn't matter where Sutter is," explained Joe Torre on pitching to Ken Oberkfell in the ninth inning.

Joe Torre did move the faster Brett Butler to center field as a defensive replacement moving Dale Murphy to left field where Torre thought Murphy was better as an outfielder. But Murphy at 6'5" compared to the shorter Butler at 5'10", may have had the reach to get to the ball above him. "I don't know if Murphy could have caught up to the ball. The other kid [Butler] caught up to the ball; he just couldn't reach it," explained Joe Torre in comparing the intricacies of Murphy versus Butler and the chances of making the difficult catch.

Dale Murphy did not argue the call by the manager. "He [Butler] said he just barely missed it. It might have been three feet further away because he is faster," Murphy said. "I don't think I'd have gotten it."

Taking Phil Niekro out of the game after six innings may have revealed some growing negativity on the part of Niekro about the way that Torre, as a manager, was handling his former teammate. "I got what I wanted out of Phil. We had the lead going into the seventh and a chance to score more runs," explained Torre after replacing Niekro in the lineup with the pinch-hitting Biff Pocoroba, with runners on first and second with one out in the seventh. "I wasn't looking for a complete game from Niekro or anyone else with my bullpen," said Torre.

But Torre may have been worried that Niekro was nursing an injury that would further reduce his chances as a hitter in the seventh inning situation. "They hit a couple of balls hard off Phil the inning before, and my secret agent told me his thumb [injured batting in the Wednesday rainout] was bothering him," explained Torre.

Phil Niekro, however, was not willing to concede anything to his manager during his post-game comments:

The thumb wasn't bothering me any more when he took me out of the game than when I was warming up before the game. When I get the ball, I go out to pitch nine; I wasn't surprised by the move, because he has done it throughout the year. I might understand it better if I was an absolute out at the plate.

The Atlanta Braves were going to have to win three in a row against the Cardinals to win the playoff series. It was not impossible, but not likely, even for a team capable of having long winning streaks like the 1982 Braves. Yes, the Braves won 13 in a row, but they were also a team that lost 11 games in row during the season.

The Milwaukee Brewers already did the unlikely by climbing back from a 0–2 deficit to advance to the World Series over the California Angels in the American League Championship Series. Bob Horner understood his team's losses to the Cardinals looked bad, but the Braves had come back from adversity all year. "We went through 19 losses in 21 games. I for one, am not gonna give up after two in the playoffs," said Horner on being down in the NLCS. "I'm not giving up until the last out of the last game of the last loss. We've come too far to give up now," explained Horner on his mindset going into game three.

The Atlanta Braves were going to have to defeat the ace of the Cardinals staff to get off the mat in the National League Championship Series. Joaquin Andujar, a four-time All-Star, was blossoming as one of the National League's most dominating pitchers. Although he would go on to win 20 games in 1984 and 1985, Andujar was at his best in 1982.

Andujar finished his 1982 regular season with a 15–10 win-loss record and a 2.47 ERA, and he placed in the top-five on most of the 1982 National League pitching leader statistical lists. Andujar's 1982 WAR was 5.8, which was much higher than his two 20-win seasons WAR of 3.4 and 2.2, respectively. Andujar was looking to shut the door on the Braves playoff hopes as the Cardinals rolled into Atlanta for the Sunday night game three match-up with their first trip to the World Series since 1968 on the line.

Rick Camp was going to have to be the Braves stopper on the mound and end the losing at two games. Camp had made the transition from a relief pitcher to the starting rotation by the end of 1982 after coming off dominant seasons in the Braves bullpen in 1980 and 1981, with a sub 2.00 ERA each year. Camp was so masterful as a reliever in 1981 that he placed 20th in the National League MVP Award voting in 1981. He performed admirably in 1982 with a 3.65 ERA over a career high 177 1/3 innings.

Camp came out pitching exactly like the Braves wanted as he retired the Cardinals in order in the bottom of the first inning with three groundouts. But their season was quickly coming to an end during the top of the second as Camp faced the first five batters of the inning without recording an out.

The Cardinals Keith Hernandez singled, Darrell Porter drew a walk, George Hendrick hit a single, Willie McGee rapped a triple, and Ozzie Smith hit a single to center field to put the Cardinals up 4–0 and causing Joe Torre to go to the bullpen in just the second inning with no outs.

Pascual Perez came in to stop the bleeding by retiring the side in order, but the damage was already done. The Braves were down four runs by the top of the second inning of game three, and their offense was not clicking as they could only score three runs combined in the previous 18 innings.

Bob Horner, Chris Chambliss, and Dale Murphy were the batters going into the bottom of the second, and Torre had faith his team could match the Cardinals and find a way to win. "Even when it was 4–0 after the second inning, I thought we could come back. We were able to pull off comebacks all year. We just didn't have it that night," said Torre looking back at the game over 20 years later.

A pop-fly by Horner, a groundout by Chambliss, and a Murphy strike out quickly set the tone for the game going forward as the Braves were only able to bring across two runs in 6 2/3 innings against Andujar. The Braves were able to find ways to put runners on, with 6 base hits and drawing two walks to keep the basepaths active and giving hope to the 52,173 fans at Atlanta-Fulton County Stadium. But hope was taken away as the Braves were not able to capitalize on the opportunities Andujar gave them, and the Cardinals still had Bruce Sutter up their sleeve.

"We just couldn't get the hits when we needed them most and the Cardinals were able to double us up a lot that night," explained Torre on how the game got away from the Braves as the Cardinals turned three double plays to keep the Braves from scoring more. Jerry Roster hit into two double plays, and Chambliss hit into one during game three.

Pascual Perez led the parade of five relievers as Torre was doing everything he could to keep the game within distance. Perez pitched 3 2/3 innings, only allowing an earned run before giving way for Donnie Moore with two outs in the top of the fifth inning.

Andujar entered the bottom of the seventh, allowing no runs, and only giving up two hits. But the Braves were about to make some noise and get Andujar out of the game. Back-to-back base hits by Claudell Washington and Bob Horner set up Chris Chambliss with runners on first and third with no outs and a chance to get the Braves back in the game. Terry Harper was at third as a pinch runner for Washington, and he was able to score on a groundball by Chambliss as the Cardinals traded a run for a double play.

The Braves still had a little more in their tank as Murphy kept the pressure on Andujar by singling, advancing to second base on a wild pitch, and scoring from second on a hit from Glenn Hubbard to make the game 5–2. The Braves were finally able to knock Andujar out of the game, but that meant bringing Bruce Sutter in. Sutter quickly got out of the inning with a fly ball for the third out.

Rick Mahler and Steve Bedrosian worked through trouble on the mound for the Braves, giving up two hits and an error, leaving three Cardinals on base during the top of the eighth inning to keep it 5–2, but Sutter—using his splitfinger to perfection—tossed three groundouts during the top of the eighth inning. Garber then took the mound for the Braves in the top of the ninth allowing Willie McGee to hit a solo home run to make it 6–2 with Terry Harper, Bob Horner, and Chris Chambliss as the last hope to turn the game around for the bottom of the ninth inning.

Sutter went three up and three down as the Braves lost the game 6–2, lost the series 3–0, and were sent home from their first postseason since 1969.

For the Atlanta Braves, their big bats simply disappeared in the National League Championship Series. The Braves who had led the National League in home runs were kept in the park all series. The Braves could only muster 15 hits, for a .169 batting average, a .219 on-base percentage accounting for five runs across their three games. The Saint Louis Cardinals pounced on the Braves with 34 hits, a .330 batting average, and a .395 on-base percentage.

In October, we often see good pitching beating good batting. For the Cardinals, this held true as their three starting pitchers only allowed four earned runs to the Braves, and their bullpen was hardly touched as the Cardinals used just two relievers with Doug Bair pitching just one inning, and Bruce Sutter pitching 4 1/3 innings allowing zero runs. The starting rotation for the Braves had been suspect all season, except for Phil Niekro, not being able to go deep into games and forcing Joe Torre to have to rely on the bullpen, but the luck finally ran out in the NLCS as the overworked bullpen couldn't save them.

The starting pitching was only able to go 12 1/3 innings, forcing the Braves to use relievers early and often, like going to Pascual Perez in just the second inning of the deciding game. The Braves bullpen allowed 23 runners to reach base across their 13 innings pitched for seven runs. The three starting pitchers went 12 1/3 innings pitched and allowed 10 runs to score. For the NLCS, the

Saint Louis Cardinals pitched to a sparkling 1.33 ERA, and the Braves were a ghastly 6.04 ERA.

Cardinals manager Whitey Herzog knew it was his pitching that made all the difference as they held Horner, Chambliss, and Murphy to four hits in 32 at-bats. "Good pitching beats good hitting every time," explained Herzog. "We were able to shut down the middle of the batting order, those mashers that led the National League in homers. That was the difference," said Herzog as he would soon go on to beat the Milwaukee Brewers in the World Series over seven games with the same results.

The Cardinals worked through the National League leader in home runs—the Braves at 146—but the Brewers smashed a Herculean 216 home runs for the year in the American League, leading baseball by 30 home runs and scoring a baseball best 891 runs.

"Now that the season is over and I can reflect," said Joe Torre after the loss, "I can be happy that we played our hearts out all season. The guys learned a lot about themselves. Without a pitching rotation, I think we did a heck of a job," continued Torre, touching on an area needing to be improved for the 1983 season.

Torre, although proud of what the team accomplished, knew that something had to change with the team going forward. Pitching was the top of the list, left-handed specifically. "That is one of the things we are going to have to get," explained Torre after game three. "We need left-handed pitching desperately. The pitching staff has been patch-work from the beginning, so I guess we were lucky to go as far as we did."

In a little-known fun fact, and of little importance, is that Ted Turner caught two foul balls during the 1982 National League Championship Series. One ball in Saint Louis and another in Atlanta, were not the mementos that Turner and the Braves wanted going into the offseason, but baseball in Atlanta was on the precipice of greatness.

8

1983 As the Favorites

The Atlanta Braves were going into the 1982 offseason with high expectations for the 1983 season as Dale Murphy and Joe Torre were receiving trophies and accolades for their breakthroughs to Major League Baseball's most elite levels for a player and a manager, respectively.

Dale Murphy earned honors and accomplishments in 1982:

- Second NL All-Star selection
- First Associated Press All-Star selection
- First Sporting News All-Star selection
- First NL Gold Glove Award
- First NL Most Valuable Player Award (2 total)
- First Sporting News Player of the Year Award
- First NL Silver Slugger Award (4 total)
- Member of the 20/20 club (20 home runs and 20 stolen bases)
- Third Braves player to appear in all 162 regular season games

This was the first MVP Award for a Braves player since the great Hank Aaron earned it in 1957. The always humble Murphy took the accolades in stride. "I think it was more a tribute to how our team did," said Murphy after receiving 14 of 24 MVP first place votes. "Our team doing that well is really the reason I was being considered," continued Murphy on winning the 1982 National League MVP.

Joe Torre was named the 1982 National League Manager of the Year by the Associated Press with Torre receiving 35 of the 79 votes cast by a nationwide panel of sports writers. Frank Robinson of the San Francisco Giants placed second, followed by the Cardinals Whitey Herzog for third place.

Torre already had a full shelf of trophies as a player, but receiving an award as a manager was not something he was expecting as the Atlanta Braves manager, and he was glad to make room for the hardware. "It's very satisfactory and kind of funny going from getting fired a year ago, to Manager of the Year," said Torre, remembering he had been fired by the 1981 New York Mets. "This has to compare with winning the 1971 Most Valuable Player Award, but I like this one a little better because we finished first. When I won the MVP, we finished second," explained Torre showing the same team-first attitude as his MVP player, Murphy.

Team owner Ted Turner was happy to add a year extension to Torre's contract after the team won the National League West, and he seemed as happy that it was at the expense of Herzog and the Cardinals. "It's just terrific. I couldn't be more happy," Turner said at the time. "He [Torre] beat out Whitey Herzog. That's great. I'm just tickled to death."

Joe Torre remembers getting the extension as a reward for winning the 1982 NLCS during a trip to Turner's South Carolina plantation during the offseason. Most of the trip was not about a contract extension, it was about the manager and owner spending time alone in an environment Torre was not used to.

"I was woken up at 4 in the morning to go bird, deer hunting, all of that kind of stuff during the trip. I was a kid from Brooklyn, so I am not familiar with all that stuff," explained Torre during an interview for this book. "On the first day, before I even got in the house, he gave me a rifle and put me in a deer stand. It was funny, I was not going to shoot anything, but I stayed up there for a bit before I came down and went in the house."

Seeing Turner behind the wheel of a boat was something Torre still remembers fondly. "We did go in the marsh for hunting, we were on a boat, and I remember that it got really rough, and he took over from the captain and quieted the boat down. Looking at him steering it he showed me that side of him that won the America's Cup," said Torre on seeing the 1977 America's Cup Skipper.

Even as the accolades were coming in, Ted Turner was busy signing checks, contract extensions, and a free agent or two in an effort to keep the Braves moving in a winning direction. In just two contract extensions, Turner put out more money than the $12 million he paid for the Braves in 1976.

Turner had the money and was going to try to keep his homegrown stars in Atlanta. Even the one he often feuded with who had vowed to never resign.

After thinking about trading All-Star third baseman, Bob Horner, the Braves signed Horner to a four-year contract worth $5 million; they signed Dale Murphy to a five-year $8 million contract; and Glenn Hubbard received a five-year $2 million contract. With the three young centerpieces of the team locked up, the Braves and Phil Niekro mutually agreed to go year to year starting with a one-year $800,000 contract. Other key additions were starting pitcher Pete Falcone and reliever Terry Forster.

Turner also knew how to build provisions into contracts to further motivate his two biggest stars: Murphy's salary went up each year of the five years starting with $1.3 million, $1.5 million, $1.6 million, $1.8 million, and $1.9 million, and included bonuses totaling another $350,000 each year for Most Valuable Player, All-Star team, and if the Braves made the World Series; Murphy would also get $100,000 if the Braves attendance went to 2.2 million. There was also a yearly salary deferment of 10 percent interest to be paid over a 25-year period starting at retirement.

For Bob Horner, the incentive was more of a gut check. Horner would be required to weigh himself 13 times over the regular season, and each time he weighed 215 pounds or less, he would get $7,692.31. The total would be added to his $900,000 base salary potentially making his salary $1 million for the season.

Torre did the Friday weigh-ins when the Braves played at home but didn't really think Horner understood why it was happening. "It was not really about whatever number the contract came up with, it was just about Bob taking better care of himself, and maybe not getting hurt as much," explained Torre during an interview for the book, while remembering Horner wearing rubber shirts to try to get the weight off just before the weigh-ins.

Going into the 1983 season, the Braves were taking shape with high hopes as the defending NL West Champions. Manager Torre had an extended contract and with young cornerstones of the franchise in place for years to come, as well as a young lineup on the right side of 30 years old, Torre should have been feeling secure in his and the team's future. But he wasn't. As a long-time player and now as a manager going into his eighth year, he knew better than to be complacent.

"I always felt as a player and of course as a manger I still knew you had to prove yourself every day. You are always looking to get better. I never really could look down the road much, but I was excited going forward after the 1982 team," said Torre.

Torre understood that pitching was going to be key to the sustained excellence of a winning Atlanta Braves franchise. "Pitching is always the main part of a team, and we had some young pitching, and some good veterans. Gene Garber in the bullpen, Steve Bedrosian was coming along, I was hoping we could get to the promised land," said Torre. "The 1982 team was so streaky, but we learned from each other. I felt good for the 1983 chances."

But a cold reality of baseball hit Torre at the beginning of spring training in 1983. "You're always optimistic when you come into spring training, but I still remember sitting with Paul Snyder who was the farm director at the time. He said there were a lot of people who didn't want to hire me. He didn't want me as manager either (at the time of the 1982 hiring). It was just strange," said Torre.

But Torre did remember Snyder saying, "I don't think anybody else could have done what you did with last year's team."

For his part, Torre took it as Snyder going to bat for the 1982 managerial candidates who were already part of the Braves franchise. After all, Torre had his own trusted coaches, like Bob Gibson, and a network with Chris Chambliss and Bob Watson, built through an earned mutual respect and loyalty. "I told Paul that I understood, and I took it as he was in charge of the minor leagues and he should want his people to get an opportunity to manage," said Torre. But the reality is that it may have planted some seeds of doubt in the next year or two. "It was just it wasn't totally comfortable for me after that," explained Torre, who would manage only two more years for the Braves.

The Braves' starting rotation was falling into place with the 1983 Braves rolling out the hopefully improved pitching staff of Phil Niekro, Rick Camp, rookie Craig McMurtry, Pascual Perez, and free agent addition Pete Falcone as the fifth starter.

The 1983 Opening Day lineup for the Braves did not change much from 1982, except Brett Butler started in center field, and an unhappy Jerry Royster was a utility player, rather than a regular starter:

1 Brett Butler, centerfield

2 Rafael Ramirez, shortstop

3 Claudell Washington, rightfield

4 Dale Murphy, leftfield

5 Bob Horner, third base

6 Chris Chambliss, first base

7 Glenn Hubbard, second base

8 Bruce Benedict, catcher

9 Phil Niekro, pitcher

Torre tried Horner in the outfield during spring training. With Horner in the outfield, Jerry Royster would be the starting third baseman for the season. But Torre decided to switch Horner back to third base, which relegated Royster as a bench player and leaving him clearly unhappy as the season began. "The biggest injustice of my life," said Royster. The utility player then asked for a trade for the third time, after making similar requests in 1980 and 1981, each time after learning he would not leave spring training as a starter.

The Braves general manager knew the value of a player like Royster and quickly denied the gifted player his trade request. "I told Jerry, maybe I am selfish, but I like to have good players on my team, and I am not going to trade you," said John Mullen to Royster about his trade request. "The only way I'd trade Jerry Royster is if I was under orders from Mr. Turner to do so, and I'm not," explained Mullen about Royster, who finally signed in free agency with the Padres after the 1984 season.

The Braves did not win their Opening Day game, losing 5–4 to the Cincinnati Reds and Mario Soto, so going after their 1982 opening streak was out the window, but they ripped off the first of seven wins in a row starting the next night.

The 1983 Braves came out firing on all cylinders opening April with a 14–5 win-loss record for a .737 winning percentage, good enough for the best April record in MLB for the second year in a row. But this time the Los Angeles Dodgers also were coming out hot, just a half-game behind in the NL West with a 14–6 record. The Braves were going to have to stay hot the whole season if they were going to hold off the Dodgers this year.

The month of May started out with Phil Niekro winning his first game of the year in a 2–1 retro pitching duel against the Mets and Tom Seaver at Shea Stadium in Queens, New York. As the Braves found ways to keep winning their share of games in May with a 16–12 win-loss record for a .571 winning percentage, the Dodgers were already creating space as they pulled ahead by winning 18 games and losing just eight for a .692 winning percentage for the month of May and were now 2 1/2 games up in the NL West race.

The Dodgers were not just leading the NL West in wins, they were the best in the entire National League, and well ahead of the best American League team, the Toronto Blue Jays. The Braves were the second-best team in all of baseball and couldn't even be ahead in their own division.

For Dale Murphy, the 1982 NLCS would be his only playoff experience, and he now knows just how hard it was to get there in the old playoff standard of two playoff teams in each league to make the post season. "Winning is tough. Back then you had, you just said no choice, no Wild Card, you had to win your division, you just had to do it," explained Murphy to the author during an interview for the book, comparing the pressure of winning your own division.

Over 40 years have passed since the 1982 NL West title, and Murphy is proud of being one of the last two teams in the 1982 National League. "I appreciate our 1982 team and the Division Title even more as I look back," he explained. For Murphy and his teammates looking back, the window for titles was not as large as they expected it would be. "We just expected to keep winning, but I don't think I realized necessarily just how hard it would be to keep winning and make the playoffs, and this was back in the days when it was just division winners; it is just not commonplace to win a division title," said Murphy, explaining the confidence of the 1983 Braves team.

The Braves players knew how hard it was to win the National League West in 1982, and the grueling difficulty of being a playoff team was not something they were taking for granted. They were a good young team earning their stripes and were expecting to be in the dog fight, winning their share of division titles, but they were going to have to get more from Phil Niekro who finally won his second game of the year on May 31 and was sporting a hefty 5.17 ERA in the young season.

Also, an exciting rookie pitcher was beginning to make a name for himself in the first two months of the season. Craig McMurtry, a 23-year-old pitcher, made his MLB debut on April 10, 1983, winning 4–3 over the San Diego Padres. The young rookie was the fifth Braves starter to get the ball for the season and was expected to keep the Braves close enough in games to have a chance for the bats to win, and to pitch deep into games long enough for the long season.

McMurtry took his win on April 10 and kept giving the Braves quality outings, and by the end of May he was the Braves' ace of the starting rotation with a 7–2 record with a 2.84 ERA. McMurtry and Pascual Perez were forming a formidable 1–2 pitching tandem with Perez 4–0 with a dazzling 1.74 ERA. The Braves now had some hope in the starting rotation for the future instead of the 44-year-old Phil Niekro expected to be the anchor of the staff since the 1960s.

The Braves and Dodgers both kept winning, and they finally had to play each other in the beginning of June, which would be an early test of wills for both teams and a chance to land an early punch to the mouth for either team. The Braves were winners of five of the last six games coming in, and the Dodgers were 5–2 over their last seven games.

The Braves were off to their best start in 18 years at 34–18 for the 1983 season during the first 54 games; this was 1 1/2 games better than the 1982 Braves at the same juncture. However, for Joe Torre and the Braves, it was frustrating to be winning so much and still be behind in the standings. "We feel like we've been on a treadmill," said Torre before the three-game series. "Every time we win, the Dodgers win. When they finally lose one every now and then, we fail to take advantage of it," bemoaned Torre on being 1 1/2 games behind the Dodgers before the game on June 7. "But now that we are finally going head-to-head for the first time this season, maybe we can do something about it ourselves. We know the Dodgers are the team we have to beat to repeat as division champions, we've known that since before the season even began."

The pressure would be on the Braves as they had to sweep the Dodgers to make up ground for the NL West lead. Winning two of three games would still leave the Braves half a game back, and losing all three would leave them with their backs up against the wall early in the season.

The day before the Dodgers game in the 1983 MLB Amateur Draft, the Atlanta Braves looked to the future and were able to select two players who would help them just a handful of years later when making their MLB debuts for the Braves. Ron Gant, a fourth-round pick, played seven years for the Braves starting in 1987, becoming an All-Star and MVP candidate as a main cog on the early 1990s Braves teams. Infielder Mark Lemke was drafted as a 27th-round pick, making his Braves debut in 1988 and playing for the Braves for 10 MLB seasons including the 1995 World Series Championship team. The Braves were starting to look to the future, but playing the Dodgers was the clear and present danger.

The three-game series was lining up nicely for the Braves rotation with Pascual Perez (6–1) against Bob Welch (4–4), Rick Camp (5–4) against Fernando Valenzuela (6–2), and Craig McMurtry (7–2) against Burt Hooton (4–2).

The Braves' bats were showing up too, as they had four players in the lineup hitting .300 or better, but it was Dale Murphy who was the titan, leading the National League at the time with 13 home runs, 43 RBIs, and 50 runs.

The Braves were able to draw first blood as Pascual Perez dominated seven innings, allowing one run and bringing his record to 7–1. Steve Bedrosian pitched two scoreless frames for his eighth save of the year in the 4–1 Braves victory, bringing the Braves within a half game of first place.

The Wednesday night game was an 11–5 Dodgers victory with neither Fernando Valenzuela nor Rick Camp pitching particularly effectively. Both teams homered three times, and the Dodgers were able to put their lead back to 1 1/2 games.

The rubber game of the three-game series had the developing Braves ace, Craig McMurtry, on the mound pitching well, going 6 1/3 innings and allowing only one earned run. But the Braves never held the lead in the game, finally losing 4–1 after their bullpen uncharacteristically gave up three runs during the eighth inning, allowing the Dodgers to snap a 1–1 for the eventual victory.

Even though the Braves lost two of three games, the Atlanta fans came out to the park and cheered in record numbers. The 132,836 fans were the most for a three-game series in the Braves franchise history of 108 years to date.

The June 2 to June 12 homestand was a chance to see how the Braves stacked up against their main competition in the National League West, the Los Angeles Dodgers and the San Francisco Giants, as well as the World Series Champion Saint Louis Cardinals.

The Braves were able to beat the Cardinals three out of four games with a combined 19-8 drubbing, but after losing two of three to the Dodgers, the Braves were only able to split the four games with the San Francisco Giants to bring their homestand to a pedestrian 6-5 win-loss record. The Braves then took a cross-country flight to begin a two-week road trip starting on the West Coast in Los Angeles for three games, and then going to San Francisco for three more against the Giants, concluding a brutal 13 consecutive games against their bitter National League West rivals.

The Dodgers and Braves traded wins with pitcher's duels for a 4-3 Braves loss and a 3-2 Braves win, before a 6-1 Braves loss in game three gave the Los Angeles Dodgers two of three again and set the tone against the Braves by beating them 4 out of 6 games.

The trip to Candlestick Park was not kind to the Braves either, as the San Francisco Giants swept the Braves for three games, bringing the Braves to 2-5 against them.

The pressure test at roughly a third of the way through the season was not a good sign for the Atlanta Braves; they played the best of the National League during the last 17 games both at home and on the road with a healthy Braves team intact with both Bob Horner and Dale Murphy in the lineup and hitting well, yet the Braves were able to only go 7-10. Even more alarming for their NL West Division hopes, the Braves only went 4-9 against the Dodgers and Giants sinking from 2 1/2 games back to 5 1/2 games behind the Los Angeles Dodgers.

This deficit was the most the Braves were behind all season against the Dodgers. The Braves were not able to trade blows with their arch enemies, who were able to square up and knock the Braves down.

But as the Baseball Gods can sometimes do, they smiled upon the Braves as their next legs were through Houston for the Astros and then Cincinnati to face the Reds, allowing the Braves to get up off the mat and then play the Astros and Reds again in Atlanta to start off June. The 15-game stretch from June 24 to July 4 would allow the Braves to feast on the bottom two teams in the NL West, with the Braves taking advantage of the opportunity and going 11–4. Most importantly, this allowed the Braves to wipe away the Los Angeles 5 1/2 game lead as the Dodgers lost 10 of 14 games, surging all the way to a one game lead for the Atlanta Braves in a stunning 6 1/2 game swing in two weeks going into the All-Star break.

Once again, the Atlanta Braves had Major League Baseball's best record at the All-Star break, this time at 49–31 with a .617 winning percentage. The 1983 Braves team rolled into the break with a superior winning percentage over the 1982 Braves, who had .607. So, 1983 looked like an even better model than the 1982 title-winning model. "We had a great team in 1982, but on paper our 1983 team could have been even better," explained Dale Murphy on how the two teams compare to him years later.

But being on top at the All-Star break was not a reason for a celebration, and Joe Torre knew it. "It's a lot like a lap time at the Indianapolis 500. Nobody cares how long you've led when you get around to the finish line," explained Torre going into the All-Star break with his team on top in the National League.

But history appeared to be pointing toward good things for the 1983 Braves as they checked off at least 50 wins by the 81–game point of the season and were on top of the division at the All-Star break. Going into 1983, 33 of the 52 teams leading the division at the break won their division (the 1969 and 1982 Braves did). Of 29 teams to win 50 of their first 81 games, only six did not make the playoffs. But, as they say, it is baseball.

The Braves continued to win in July as they won the most games they would win in any month in 1983. They went 18–11 with a .621 winning percentage, and this would also be their top offensive month scoring 153 runs, almost 20 more runs than their next most productive, the 135 runs they scored in June.

After beating the San Francisco Giants 8–3 on the road, the Braves commanded a 6 1/2 game lead over the Los Angeles Dodgers and were appearing to be running away with the National League West on August 1.

The positivity continued as the Braves crushed the San Francisco Giants 8–1 to raise their record to 67–42 on August 4. It was the first time since coming to Atlanta in 1966 that the Braves were 25 games above the .500.

The Braves were enjoying the season up until August 15 with a 5 1/2 game lead. It wasn't the 4–0 loss to the San Diego Padres that was going to take the air out of the season. It was Bob Horner suffering a season-ending wrist injury that played a large role in the Braves 1983 demise. Horner was hitting as well as Dale Murphy, hitting .303 with 20 home runs as the Braves tandem were pounding National League pitchers.

Unlike the 1982 Braves team that went on an incredible 13-game winning streak to start the season and following it up with an incredible 11-game losing streak that pushed the team to the brink of disaster in August, the 1983 team was not that roller coaster of a team. They only could win seven in a row at their best and kept their longest losing streak to a modest six games.

The 1983 team also suffered an August collapse, but it was not a nosedive off a cliff, it was a slow descent, almost controlled chaos, resulting in the Braves up a season high 6 1/2 games over the Dodgers on August 13, and then 14 games later, the Braves were out of first place.

The 1983 Braves went 5–9 over those games to lose their National League West lead, and they never got it back. The 1983 team did not follow a long-sustained August losing streak like the 11-game losing streak of the 1982 Braves; rather, the 1983 team did not perform the way it was expected to.

On August 28, 1983, the Atlanta Braves looked to shore up their starting rotation by trading for former All-Star Len Barker from the Cleveland Indians and giving away two future star players Brett Butler and Brook Jacoby. In a strange move, however, the Braves retained the agreed-upon traded players until the season ended.

Barker, 8–13, with a 5.11 ERA at the time of the trade quickly agreed to a five-year, $4.5 million contract making him one of the highest paid players in baseball. But this trade didn't pay off like it had for the team in 1969 when the Braves were aiming for the 1969 NL West title and acquired a 45-year-old Hoyt Wilhelm, who was able to get two wins, four saves, and struck out 14 batters in 12 innings, thereby helping the Braves take the National League West. Barker was only able to go 1–3 down the stretch for the Braves, and he failed to pay off for the long-term as he was often injured during his three years in Atlanta, only winning 10 games while losing 30 with a 4.64 ERA.

The 1983 Braves went 12–16 in August with the longest losing streak being four games. They also did not have any winning streaks with their longest August run of three wins in a row against the Cubs on August 19–21. Win a game, lose three; win two, lose three more. It all added up to death by a thousand paper cuts. It was a trend the Braves carried through September, winning 11 games and losing 16 down the stretch.

By September 23, the Braves were 5 1/2 games back and limping into the offseason losing two of three to the Padres to finish second in the NL West, three games behind the Dodgers with a record of 88–74.

9

The Impatience of the 1984 Offseason

On September 25, 1983, 11 members of the front office, coaches, and Ted Turner were already looking to 1984 and how their starting pitching could shake out. For the first time in decades, they decided they would not have Phil Niekro as part of the Braves plans. Joe Niekro believes it was Joe Torre or pitching coach Bob Gibson who wanted Phil gone, but the decision was framed at the time as looking to the future and giving the young pitchers more of an opportunity.

"It wasn't just manager Joe Torre, or pitching coach Bob Gibson," according to the general manager John Mullen. "The vote was unanimous that it would be in the best interest of the Braves to have a young starter such as Ken Dayley replace Niekro in the starting rotation. True, Niekro won 11 games last season, but Dayley probably would have won eleven or more if he had made 31 starts," explained Mullen on why the Braves released long-time Atlanta Braves pitcher Niekro.

Turner told Niekro in early October, shortly after the season ended, about the Braves' intentions to not have him in the starting rotation for the 1984 season, but Turner offered Niekro several options for him to remain with the Braves, either as player or in another capacity.

Turner wanted to move Niekro to a front office job, or perhaps to a manager's role with a minor league team, or if Niekro did not want to retire as a player, he could stay on as a relief pitcher or even come into 1984 spring training and win a job in the rotation. There were opportunities, but Niekro wanted to keep pitching as a starter and asked for his release from the team to pursue options elsewhere.

Niekro was not going to burn bridges, but it seemed like he was keeping the matches in his pocket in case he decided to light it up. "I wasn't about to go to spring training holding Ted's hand and pitching in his shadow," said Niekro. "I'm convinced I can still win as a starting pitcher and help some team win a pennant. But the Braves did not want me back. The manager, coaches, and front office made that clear. I appreciate Ted's offers and sometime in the future I may work for the Braves again," explained Niekro on why he asked for his unconditional release from the Braves.

Phil Niekro went on to sign with the New York Yankees during the offseason going 16–8 with a 3.09 ERA and making his fifth, and final, All-Star team for the 1984 Yankees. He was able to get his 300th win on the final day of the 1985 season pitching for the Yankees.

The Braves and Niekro were able to agree on a $1 contract for Niekro to start the final home game of the 1987 season. Niekro pitched until the top of the fourth inning, exiting the game with no outs, bases loaded, with the Braves leading 5–2 against the San Francisco Giants. Chuck Cary was called into the game to try to keep the Braves in the lead. As usual Niekro tried to stay in the game but was overruled by the Braves manager, Chuck Tanner. Cary's first batter, Candy Maldonado, launched a grand slam. The Braves eventually lost the game 15–6, falling to 20 games below .500 at 67–87.

Even after Joe Torre put together back-to-back winning seasons, and perhaps even having a better, more consistent team in 1983 than in 1982, there was already noise that he should be replaced as manager, but Ted Turner was not allowing any of that talk—at least not in the media.

The criticisms of Torre were that he was not properly handling the bullpen, not sufficiently motivating the players, and failing at baseball strategy. There was also a backlash by fans and the media, blaming Torre for driving Niekro out of town.

The 1983 Braves team ran out steam as they were 39–43 after the All-Star break, with a 17–28 record the last seven weeks of the season. Turner did not feel that Torre was the reason for the team not making the playoffs. "We were disappointed we didn't win the division, but Joe didn't do us wrong," said Turner in October of 1983. He even compared the team favorably to the other 1982 postseason teams. "Every division winner from last year finished fourth or worse this year. Except us, we placed second and were the last team in baseball to be eliminated."

Turner even mildly scolded those who doubted Torre as the Braves manager. "Boy, how fast people forget around here. Joe is a proven winner. Heck, he was Manager of the Year last year," said Turner to critics of Torre after the 1983 season.

The 1983 Braves were in first place for 83 games in the 1983 season, but the last game in first was all the way back on August 28 leaving the fans feeling the Braves were not on the ascent going into 1984. Could they double down and keep the team winning, and even make it over the Dodgers or other tough teams in the NL West in 1984?

The Braves, as always, were looking for the starting rotation to be strong enough to give their big bats the opportunity to keep out in front and win games, but Pascual Perez threw a screwball into the works in January of 1984. Perez was arrested on January 9 in his native country of the Dominican Republic on drug charges, and he spent three months in a Dominican prison, leaving his role with the Braves and his future in baseball very much in question. But the Braves still had Len Barker, Craig McMurtry, and Ken Dayley ready to go.

Torre was not ready to give an inch going into the 1984 season with the Perez arrest and Claudell Washington just getting out of rehabilitation for drug dependency. "I have no control over such things" said Joe Torre in early February 1984. "But I certainly don't see this as the end of the world for us," continued Torre, trying to keep the team playing well for the 1984 season. But even more cracks were evident with the Braves players on the field as two of them got into fight in the outfield before a spring training game in March.

"I don't want anyone to think we're going to let it go," said Torre after the fight between Bob Horner and Bruce Benedict. But the manager downplayed the incident between the players. "You can have a fight anywhere. Why should ballplayers be any different?"

Horner at the time refused to let on what the fight was about, only saying, "It's none of your business, It's a personal thing. We'll settle it our own way." Benedict only went as far as to call it a "family squabble."

The good vibes from the underdog 1982 team were now vanishing as adversity piled on to the players entering the 1984 season:

- The Braves offered Richard "Goose" Gossage a $5.5 million contract over five years, only to be spurned in favor of the San Diego Padres.
- Tommy Boggs, the young pitcher who was upset to be passed over for a start in game two in the 1982 NLCS was released.
- The trade for Len Barker was completed when Brett Butler, Brook Jacoby, and Rick Behenna were sent by the Braves to the Cleveland Indians to complete the August deal.
- Len Barker signed with the Braves for $4 million over five years.

The Braves did not begin with the usual hot April start that had occurred in each year previously under Joe Torre's tenure. In 1984, the Braves had a 2–7 record on April 13 and finished April with a 9–12 win-loss record.

By May 10, after a 7–3 victory by Len Barker over the Mets, the Braves were finally at .500. They continued to play well in May as they were able to go 17–11 for the month with a winning percentage of .607. Even with a good month, the

Braves were looking up at the standings to see the Los Angeles Dodgers up by two games, the Goose Gossage San Diego Padres a half-game behind Los Angeles, and the Cincinnati Reds tied for third place with the Braves. It was only a game, but two months into the season there were four teams clawing at each other for the title with barely any separation.

The Braves appeared to be getting hot, taking the division lead by winning their first eight games in June, taking over first place on June 2 for the first time all season with a 9–3 win from the recently returned Pascual Perez winning his fifth game since his start of the season on May 7.

Perez continued his dazzling start after his Dominican prison stay with an 8–1 complete game victory over Dodgers rookie right-hander Orel Hershiser, to bring the first place Braves to a 34–23 record. The Braves had pulled a remarkable turnaround going 32–16 since April 14. This was not going to last, however, as the 11 games over .500 would be their best winning percentage for the rest of the year.

Unfortunately for the Braves, this would prove to be the high-water mark for the season. Atlanta lost five in a row from June 8 to 12 to fall into second place, 3 1/2 games out of first. They were never to be in first place again in 1984. A Dodgers walk-off victory over the Braves on June 9 ushered the San Diego Padres into first place replacing the Braves atop the National League West.

The Braves would struggle the rest of the year to not only chase the San Diego Padres, but also to try to stay at .500 or better for the year. As June ended with a 17–12 record for the month, the Braves were still very much in the race at only three games behind the Padres with a 43–35 win-loss record, and the Dodgers were hanging around at 5 1/2 games back.

While the Braves were falling out of first place within eight days in June, they were making another step to secure their future as they selected Tom Glavine in the second round as the 47th overall pick of the 1984 June Amateur Draft. Glavine burned through the minor leagues, making his Braves debut in 1987; he pitched for 22 years in his Hall of Fame pitching career, winning

244 games for the Braves and topping the 300-victory mark with 305 wins. Combined with the 1983 MLB Draft of Ron Gant and Mark Lemke, the Braves now were developing three core members who would be taking baseball by storm starting in 1991.

The Braves had had the best record in baseball at the All-Star breaks during 1982 and 1983 under Torre, but 1984 saw the Braves at a pedestrian 46–41 record but still in contention in the NL West, five games behind the upstart San Diego Padres. The Padres were led by playoff warriors such as Graig Nettles, Goose Gossage, and Steve Garvey, along with Tony Gwynn, who was becoming one of the best hitters in the National League in 1984, and wouldn't let up until his retirement in 2001.

Without Bob Horner in the lineup due to injury, the Braves were not mashing as much. Without Phil Niekro, the starting rotation had too many holes to fill as Craig McMurtry was not able to replicate the mastery of his 1983 rookie season.

The Braves could only go 12–16 for the month of July, unable to take first place back, but they were able to stay in second place as the Padres were beginning to run away in the National League West. Going into August, the Padres were up 8 1/2 games over the Braves and 12 games up on the Dodgers. The Braves were still battling as one of the only five teams at the .500 mark or better going into August.

The Braves were not a winning team from August 1 to the end of the season as they went 25–31, earning the least number of victories from August 1 out of all the teams in the National League West. The 182 runs over the final 56 games were by far the worst in Major League Baseball with the Boston Red Sox leading baseball with 323, and the Chicago Cubs easily leading the Braves by 85 runs. The Braves pitching staff pitched respectably enough, allowing 223 runs for fifth-least runs allowed. But the Braves offense finally deserted the team as the pitching held up to end 1984.

Their August record of 11–17 helped dip them below .500 on August 28 where they would remain until a run of winning four out of five games had them at 79–78. The Braves promptly lost four of their next five games to finish the season with an 80–82 record, good enough to tie for second place with the Houston Astros, 12 games out from the San Diego Padres, who went on to win the NLCS over the Chicago Cubs. The Padres lost the World Series in five games to the Detroit Tigers, led by Jack Morris, Alan Trammell, and Kirk Gibson.

The Braves were now not just battling the Los Angeles Dodgers; the San Diego Padres and the Houston Astros announced themselves as teams that may be better than the Braves going forward.

10

The Braves Turn Left

Was this a time for patience and to allow Joe Torre–who had been so successful in bringing the Braves such high expectations–the opportunity to right the ship?

Torre, for one, believed he would be back. But cracks between the front office and Torre were perhaps larger than he believed, as the team looked to organize their 1985 team. "I thought I should be back, why wouldn't I think so?" explained Torre, looking back during the writing of this book. "We had so much adversity and change, but we were still contenders for the year. But I knew maybe I wouldn't make it back."

The year 1984 was disappointing for Joe Torre, but he still believed the Braves could be the preseason favorite in the NL West if they could finally get left-handed pitchers. "That's the most disappointing of all. It takes time to put something together. I think next year we would have gone into spring training… with the feeling we were going to win this thing," explained Torre, on being fired after the 1984 season.

The Braves front office had wanted to hire long-time Braves minor league manager Eddie Haas to be the 1982 Braves manager, and they were now finally going to get their way after Ted Turner had overruled them and opted to bring in Torre in 1982. The groundwork was in play during the 1984 season with Haas being added to the coaching staff with two months to go in the season and being asked to assess the team for the front office.

Torre thinks there was a disconnect between the front office and his coaches, like pitching coach Bob Gibson, or the second pitching coach, Rube Walker. "The front office did not want Bob Gibson back for 1985. I felt some pressure on that during the year, but I was not about to get rid of my guys," explained a loyal Torre. "I knew they really like Mazzone." The Braves announced Johnny Sain and Leo Mazzone as the pitching coaches at the time of the Haas announcement.

Many years later, Torre believes that maybe the team thought they had gotten as far as they could with him at the helm and needed someone new to take the team to the next level after finishing first, second, and second. "Maybe they just thought I was getting stale to the players, and they were not responding to me the same way anymore," said Torre.

The Braves were a team trying to utilize the younger players whom Haas had such a big hand in developing the past several years. In 1984, 19 of the 40 players on the Braves roster had played for Haas as their manager at some point. Maybe he could be the answer to the Braves future success, since the front office believed in their minor league system developing players, and Haas was MLB-ready as well.

Perhaps it was a sign of Turner's own belief, but Haas was offered only a one-year contract to manage the team instead of the three-year contract Torre had received when he was hired as manager. By late August 1985, Haas would find out if he was going to get another year to develop the team that he and the front office gave him so much credit for.

The 1985 Braves offseason was earth shattering for Braves fans as they signed Saint Louis Cardinals reliever Bruce Sutter to a six-year contract, paying Sutter $4.8 million and another $4.8 million in deferred payments at 13 percent interest, payable each year for 30 years at $1.3 million per year. After missing out on Goose Gossage for 1984, Turner signed his man.

Cardinals manager Whitey Herzog commented on losing Sutter. "To me, Bruce is the best there ever was," Herzog said. "Losing him is like Kansas

City losing Dan Quisenberry.... I told Bruce, 'Look, you've taken care of your children and your grandchildren and your great-grandchildren. Now, if I get fired in July, will you take care of me and Mary Lou?'"

The 1985 Braves team came out hot with Eddie Haas at the helm going 4–1, to start the season in first place for eight days before losing first place on April 16. The Braves would not be in first place again that season, and May 1 would be their last time for the season at .500 or better. The Braves were struggling without Joe Torre.

Haas struggled with the team at 50–71, 22 games out of first place on August 25 when he was fired and replaced by Bobby Wine. The Braves responded a little better with five straight wins, but not nearly good enough as Wine went 16–25 for the rest of the season to finish the season 66–96 with a .407 winning percentage, a dramatic fall from grace for the Braves during their post Torre era as the team finished 29 games behind the first place Dodgers.

The disastrous 1985 season was capped by Sutter needing surgery on his right shoulder after his 23-save season with a bloated 4.48 ERA.

This time Ted Turner was not going to listen to his front office about what to do. Turner was determined to make some changes for the future, by bringing back a name from their past.

Long-time general manager John Mullen was now out and replaced by Bobby Cox, who was hired away from the Toronto Blue Jays. Wine, who had been asked to step in for Haas, was also let go and replaced by World Series winning manager, Chuck Tanner. Cox was flying high after leading his Toronto Blue Jays to the American League East title in 1985.

Ted Turner was the National League version of George Steinbrenner with his fourth manager in a little over a year and replacing their general manager.

As Bobby Cox served as general manager of the Braves from 1986 to 1990, the Braves started to see results from the likes of Tom Glavine, Jeff Blauser, Ron Gant, Mark Lemke, John Smoltz, Chipper Jones, David Justice, and Steve

Avery. Players like Gant, Glavine, Lemke, and Blauser had all been drafted while Joe Torre managed the team, and these players were quickly developing.

The Braves turned to the manager Torre had taken over from going into the 1982 season after having gone through managers Eddie Haas, Bobby Wine, Chuck Tanner, and Russ Nixon in just the six seasons of 1985–1990. The Braves endured six straight losing seasons without Torre before Cox had seen enough and took matters into his own hands; by June of 1990, Cox moved downstairs to the field, taking over as manager with huge results almost immediately.

The Braves went on a 14 Division Title run in just 15 seasons, with five trips to the World Series and one World Series Championship in 1995.

Even as the years fade, Bobby Wine still thinks the Braves did the wrong thing by firing Torre for Haas. "Joe Torre did a great job for that team and didn't deserve to get fired. To this day I am not sure why they did that. It certainly didn't work out well for the Braves. But Joe certainly went on to show that he was the kind of manager that could lead a team to a championship," explained Wine, a long-time friend of Torre.

Dale Murphy saw day in and day out how the team began to slip into an abyss toiling away at the bottom of the standings after Torre left. "In the 1990s, the Braves had a complete commitment to pitching; looking back I don't think our 80s teams had that commitment, or just the kind of depth you get from that," explained Murphy on how the Braves couldn't sustain their 82–84 contender run.

I'm not saying we weren't committed as a team, but we just didn't have the depth at the major league level or throughout the minor leagues and were not able to continually produce quality pitching. That's always the key to consistent success. It is key to have defense and pitching. Our offense was good and hopefully we could stay together, but we didn't stay together.

Murphy seems to think that Torre was good with the younger players, capable and willing to work with them to continue getting better. "I think our guys enjoyed playing for him. It just kind of gelled for us here with him. He wasn't there that long, only a few years, but we had our best years here with him, and many of our players had their best years with him as the manager," explained Murphy on the effect Torre had on the team.

The question must be asked, then, could the Braves have been spared years of consistent losing if they had stuck with Joe Torre instead of going to Eddie Haas? "I loved to play for Joe, and later in his career he got a chance to show what he could do with a real good team, a real good consistent team year in and year out with the Yankees. A lot of people forget Joe had some good years in Atlanta, and we were really good under him," said Murphy.

But Murphy is measured in his response when it comes to the particulars of Torre being fired. "I don't know the details of what happened with him and Ted Turner, but he [Torre] moved on," explained Murphy on the Ted Turner–Joe Torre relationship at the end of Torre's tenure.

Having a team still being a contender and going through the pain of rebuilding, like replacing a legend like Phil Niekro, is a difficult process and can easily fail. Murphy lived through it. "We just didn't have the depth to really carry on the sustained winning needed to rebuild at the same time; we tried, and it didn't work," said Murphy on the 1980s demise of the Braves. "The rebuild probably started with Smoltz, Glavine, and Kent Mercker," continued Murphy, as the rebuild began to blossom. "They really concentrated and focused on that group and rebuild."

Murphy also thought that Turner made some difficult decisions that just went wrong for the team, but once Turner began to allow Bobby Cox and others to have more control, the Braves organization began to turn the corner. As Murphy explained,

> Once John Schuerholz came in, it appeared Ted Turner took a step down from the decision making. John Shuerholz and Bobby Cox were a good team. The thing about an owner is he owns the team, so he feels like he

should be able to have some control on the team, but unfortunately, owners typically don't have what it takes to be a general manager.

Murphy would go on to discuss Joe Torre in New York, as well as other sports like the NFL as examples of the pitfalls of owner involvement in player and team decisions. "I don't know how many examples you can point to where an owner has done a good job of running a team. I think Steinbrenner tried; but I think when he finally got Brian Cashman and Joe Torre together, they were a good team," said Murphy. He added,

I think Jerry Jones is probably an example in football. It doesn't work because they don't have the expertise as much as they think they do. They gotta hire the right people and just be the CEO instead of making all the small decisions on talent. It's your scouts, your development people, and your general manager that must be making all those decisions.

Dale Murphy believes that if Joe Torre had stayed on as Braves manager, and with Bobby Cox taking over as general manager in October of 1985, there would have been an opportunity for the Braves to keep developing and wining. "John Mullen and Joe Torre had to click, and I don't think they ever really did," explained Murphy on how he perceived the Torre-Mullen relationship.

"I think Joe was able to kind of mold a group of players and personnel together. I saw him do it in Atlanta and I knew he would have it happen in New York. They [Torre and Cox] could definitely have done that in Atlanta, given the chance, but it just it wasn't to be."

11

It Had to Happen

For Joe Torre, life after managing—like for many other ex-baseball managers—led to a stop in the broadcasting booth. Torre worked as a color commentator for the California Angels and worked for NBC's Game of the Week. He was also a guest analyst for ESPN during the Earthquake World Series in 1989 between the San Francisco Giants and Oakland Athletics.

Torre, however, found his way back to the baseball dugout through an old team he used to play for, when he replaced the Cardinals Whitey Herzog, who resigned on July 6, 1990. Red Schoendienst served as acting manager for 24 games before Torre was named manager in 1990.

Torre even brought some Braves flair to the Saint Louis Cardinals, hiring some of the recently retired players to help coach. Chris Chambliss served as the 1994 hitting coach, and Dale Murphy put on the Cardinals uniform and served as a guest instructor during 1994 spring training. It was the kind of loyalty that Torre extended to those he trusted, and those relationships served him well over his career.

Torre brought winning baseball back to Saint Louis, with the Cardinals going 84–78 for second place in the 1991 NL East, 83–79 in 1992, 87–75 in 1993, 53–61–1 in 1994, and 20–27 before being fired during the 1995 season.

But then after the 1995 season, Torre's old first baseman, Bob Watson, turned Torre's career and legacy on its head.

Torre was likely not everyone's first choice to be the Yankees manager and replace Buck Showalter for the 1996 season, but the recently hired Watson was going to bat for Torre one last time, as he tapped Torre as the New York Yankees 31st manager. This turned out to be a pick that paid off for the Yankees and Torre.

For the 55-year-old, Brooklyn-born Joe Torre, it was a homecoming back to New York City where he once managed the New York Mets. He came in understanding what was expected of him in the huge media market. He was expected to win with an ownership that would often be proactive in baseball decisions. "I came to the New York Yankees after being here previously with the Mets. I managed under Ted Turner for the Braves, the Busch family in Saint Louis for the Cardinals. They were impatient to win, and I can be the same way myself," explained Torre on his mindset coming in for the Yankees in 1996.

The 1996 Yankees were looking to win their first American League East title since 1980. (The 1981 Yankees were only leading the standings at the first-half of the season to win the first-half title, ending up two games behind the second-half title winner and overall AL East–winning Milwaukee Brewers, but the Yankees went on to beat the Brewers in the ALDS and then the Oakland A's in the ALCS, thereby advancing to the 1981 World Series.) Torre was looking to repeat the magic trick of taking his team to a division title to end a long-time drought, like he had done when he led the Braves to the NL West. Torre did just that in 1996, as he led the Yankees to a 92–70 record, winning the AL East title by four games over the Baltimore Orioles.

As the Yankees were going 7–2 in the postseason, setting up their first World Series appearance since 1981, it would be against a familiar foe for Torre. The Braves had floundered badly after firing Torre before the 1985 season, having six losing seasons before a miraculous turnaround from cellar dweller in 1990 to the penthouse in 1991, making it to the World Series and being in the postseason four of the five full seasons that Bobby Cox managed.

The 1996 Braves were the defending World Series Champions after beating the Cleveland Indians in six games in 1995. The Braves were now the only baseball franchise to win a World Series in three cities (1914 Boston Braves, 1957 Milwaukee Braves, and 1995 Atlanta Braves).

The Braves were considered the heavy favorites to win the 1996 World Series after making quick work of the Los Angeles Dodgers in the National League Divisional Series, and having a thrilling series win over the Saint Louis Cardinals in the National League Championship Series.

The 1996 managers were Bobby Cox and the man who replaced him as manager beginning in 1982, Joe Torre. But for Cox, it was much more than a Torre connection. Cox had earned his first World Series ring from the New York Yankees, years before he earned one as a Brave.

Cox had a strong connection with the New York Yankees as a player and also as a manager in their minor leagues for six years. Cox was a third baseman for the New York Yankees in 1968–1969, a minor league manager from 1971 to 1976, and a coach for the 1977 World Series–winning Yankees.

The quotes from those involved in upcoming big games can often be bland, generic, and carefully crafted so as to not give bulletin board material, but Cox allowed a peek into his thoughts when asked about the Braves playing the New York Yankees before the 1996 World Series began. "Don't get me wrong, I'd love to play the Series anywhere, but it's something special here. From the midseason on, a lot of us started to wonder what would happen if we get in and the Yankees get in, and wouldn't it be great to go back to New York," he explained.

The New York Yankees pulled out all the stops with Joe DiMaggio throwing out the first pitch of the 1996 World Series. Two of the best pitchers in baseball that year were starting on the bump. The Braves John Smoltz, 24–8 during the regular season versus the Yankees Andy Pettitte, 21–8, was a pitching marquee matchup for the ages. Or it should have been.

The Atlanta Braves knocked around Pettitte and the Yankees early and often, thrashing the Yankees 12–1 in a laugh-winning game one.

In a story Torre has often told over the years, he added a funny little detail in 2024: "George Steinbrenner walked into my office and sat on my couch before Game 2 and said, 'This is a big game,' so I decided to mess with him," said Torre.

I replied to him, "George, Maddux is pitching against us. We may lose again tonight. But then we're going to Atlanta—that's my town. We'll win three there, and then next Saturday we'll come back and win the series here in New York." I then walked out of my office. I was just screwing around, making a joke, but it all happened exactly like I said it would.

Greg Maddux did indeed beat the Yankees in Game 2, tossing a 4-0 shutout and dropping the Yankees in a 0-2 hole in the World Series going into Atlanta.

If Torre had been nervous about toeing up the wrong foul ball line for the Atlanta Braves fans at home and receiving boos and jeers, he would have been wrong. The Atlanta fans gave him a returning Braves hero welcome before the Game 3 first pitch. While Torre's name was called during the lineup introductions, solid applause turned louder and louder before turning into a standing ovation for the former Braves player and manager.

Torre also was finally able to meet Jane Fonda, the famous wife of Ted Turner. "I knew that I would talk to Ted at his box before the game in Atlanta. Also, I went over to have the chance to speak with Jane Fonda," said Torre about talking with Turner at the World Series. "He told me, if the Braves couldn't win it, he would be glad if I did. I was pretty happy with that. I always thought he didn't want to fire me back then, it was more of an organizational thing and not that he didn't want me there," concluded Torre.

David Cone pitched the Yankees to a gutsy 5-2 victory while Bernie Williams hit a huge home run in the top of the eighth inning.

Game 4 was an exciting affair with both starting pitchers knocked out of the game by the sixth inning. Down 6-3 in the bottom of the eighth, the Yankees Jim Leyritz smashed a three-run home run off Mark Wohlers, tying the game at 6–6. The score would remain 6–6 until the top of the tenth when the Yankees capitalized on three walks, a hit, and an error, bringing two runs across for the eventual 8–6 Yankees victory.

Game 5 would be another chance for the pitching duel to materialize that had seemed likely for Game 1. John Smoltz and Andy Pettitte took the mound, each shutting the other team down and not allowing a run for most of the game. The only blemish was in the top of the fourth inning when Cecil Fielder hit a double to score Charlie Hayes who was on second due to an error by Marquis Grissom for an unearned run making the score 1–0. It was all the scoring needed for the pitching gem. The Yankees won 1–0 to bring the World Series back to New York knotted at 3–3.

Game 6 would be Jimmy Key versus Greg Maddux in a Game 2 matchup. The Yankees were able to draw blood against Maddux, this time with three runs in the bottom of the third inning off four hits. Those were the only runs Maddux or the Braves would allow the Yankees all game. But Key of the Yankees was able to be just a little better than Maddux for 5 1/3 innings, only allowing one run.

Torre—always one to believe in turning the lead over to the bullpen—used David Weathers, Graeme Lloyd, Mariano Rivera, and closer John Wetteland to win the game 3–2 for the Yankees' first World Series Championship since 1978.

For Torre, it was a validation. After more than 4,000 games as an MLB player and manager, he was able to win the World Series over the team he came up to the major leagues with, and the only other team that he had taken to a postseason.

For Torre, this was the first of four World Series Championships in just five years and six trips to the World Series in eight years. This was the start of a dynasty of championships for the New York Yankees from 1996 to 2000. The Yankees earned 10 American League East crowns in 12 seasons under Torre.

And Joe Torre went on to prove he could win without the Yankees by managing the Los Angeles Dodgers from 2008 to 2010 and winning back-to-back division crowns in 2008–2009 for a total of 15 division titles between three franchises.

Torre retired after the 2010 season, with 29 seasons as an MLB manager. He won 2,326 games and lost 1,997 games for a winning percentage of .538.

After the 2010 season, Bobby Cox also retired after 29 seasons. Cox managed 2,504 wins and 2,001 losses while winning five pennants and a World Series Championship. He won 15 division titles, 14 in Atlanta and one in Toronto.

The bond between the two managers should never be doubted. Their careers are forever intertwined as both danced around each other with the Atlanta Braves helping bring the Braves to a sustained prominence rarely seen among sports franchises.

Braves manager Bobby Cox wished Torre well after the final game of the 1996 World Series. "You have fun this winter," Cox said to Torre in his crowded manager's office. "You deserve it. Good going. I love you."

12

A Model Franchise

Dale Murphy knew that a general manager and the manager on the baseball field had to "click," and unluckily for John Mullen and Joe Torre—and most of all for the Braves fans—the combo of the two didn't work. Ted Turner found lightning in a bottle as Bobby Cox went back to the field and John Schuerholz took over as the general manager for the Braves. With all the new players coming up, what would become of the remaining players from the early to mid-1980s still in the lineup, like Murphy? For Murph, it was making his decision on his own terms.

As Murphy was asking for a trade from the Braves in 1990, the Braves and Cox were selecting from the 1990 MLB draft one the last essential pieces needed for sustained excellence. Chipper Jones, selected as a shortstop and number one overall pick, became one of the most beloved players in franchise history. He will forever be tied to Cox and to the Braves, having played his entire career for the Braves.

Jones was fast-tracked to the Braves, making his debut on September 11, 1993, and retiring after the 2012 season with eight All-Star selections and the 1999 National League MVP Award, as well as eventually having his number retired by the Braves, selection to the Braves Hall of Fame, and selection to Major League Baseball Hall of Fame in 2018, in his first year of eligibility, with 97.2 percent of the vote.

Murphy had been the face of the Braves during the 1980s. He knew how hard it was to stay so good for so long, as it made sense for both the player and the franchise to mutually get the most out of each other. Murphy saw his own Braves career coming to an end, and he marveled at how things were able to work out for Jones. "How many guys are like Chipper? There's only Derek Jeter, Tony Gwynn, those kinds of guys. Current-day players, it's the same it was for me in the '80s and '90s," mused Murphy.

Murphy was suffering through injuries, which took away from his playing. Certainly Murphy knew it, the front office knew it, and the fans knew it and still loved him; but clearly he didn't want a slow, sad roll out of Atlanta and spoke up to make it easier for the team deep into a rebuild.

"A lot of people don't realize that I initiated the trade from the Braves," said Murphy. "I went to Bobby [Cox] in 1990 and said I'm going to be a free agent next year," explained Murphy. "I will be leaving, I'll look at a trade if you guys want to trade me to get something back," explained Murphy on his trade veto rights. "That's how the trade with the Phillies happened."

But occasionally a player has enough homegrown credibility and oomph to stay until the end of their career with the same team. "Chipper was able to stay very productive, I couldn't do that, I always had little injuries, Glavine left, Smoltz left, organizations and players always struggle with it at the end. Freddie Freeman already left."

Baseball is an entertainment business, but bottom line, it is a business. "It is very seldom an organization will hang onto a player for sentimental reasons. It is just not done," explained Murphy on how clubs like the Braves typically let homegrown players like Phil Niekro and Bob Horner move on.

With the old making way for the new, the Braves were ready once again to take baseball by storm. Their 1991 season saw them go from the worst team in the National League to the best, winning the National League Pennant for the first time since 1958, and going on to win a record-setting 14 consecutive division titles, five National League Pennants, and a World Series championship in 1995.

In 1993, the Braves made perhaps the best free agent signing of all-time with Greg Maddux immediately paying dividends with the Braves finishing the year with 104 wins, before losing in the National League Championship to the Philadelphia Phillies.

Then 1994 saw a Major League Baseball adjustment to the divisions ultimately moving the Braves away from the Los Angeles Dodgers and the National League West and becoming part of the National League East. This realignment was to reorganize both the American and National Leagues into three divisions, the East, Central, and West, thereby introducing a Wild Card Playoff spot in each league for the postseason.

The 1994 season was the first for the Braves in the realigned NL East, but the season was canceled on August 11 because of the 1994–1995 Major League Baseball Strike.

The Braves came back in 1995 to win their first NL East crown, and they went on to win the World Series that year against the Cleveland Indians. The Atlanta Braves would win 11 straight NL East titles from 1995 to 2005, winning National League titles in 1996 and 1999, but they lost the World Series both years to Joe Torre and his New York Yankees.

Then in October 1996, the Ted Turner era came to an end, as Time Warner acquired the Turner Broadcasting System for nearly $8 billion, including the Braves franchise. The Braves and Bobby Cox kept winning until 2006, when the team went 79–83 to finish third in the NL East and was out of the playoffs for the first time since 1990. The 2005 NL East title would prove to be the last for Cox as manager, with the Braves missing the playoffs for four straight years. The Braves would finish below .500 again in 2008 with a 72–90 record. Cox took the Braves to the postseason for his final time in 2010, earning a Wild Card and losing to the Houston Astros three games to one in the National League Divisional Series.

Fredi Gonzalez took over as manager starting in the 2011 season, leading the Braves to back-to-back second-place finishes with 89 and 94 wins. The 94-win season in 2012 earned the Braves a Wild Card spot in the playoffs, losing in the National League Wild Card Series to the Saint Louis Cardinals. The Braves returned atop the NL East in 2013, going 96–66 but losing to the Los Angeles Dodgers 3–1 in the five-game National League Divisional Series.

The Braves suffered through losing seasons 2014–2017 with three consecutive 90-plus loss seasons. Then after a short rebuild, the Atlanta Braves reloaded and fired off six straight division crowns with Brian Snitker from 2018 to 2023, highlighted by returning to the top of the Major League Baseball mountain and winning the 2021 World Series in six games against the Houston Astros.

The Braves were finally World Series champs for the first time since 1995, a total gap of 25 years. Once the Braves were up 2–0 against Joe Torre and the Yankees in the World Series, but Torre and the Yankees beat the Braves for six consecutive games combined in the 1996 and 1999 World Series.

Joe Torre finally saw his Braves career come full circle with his induction into the Braves Hall of Fame in 2022. Eight years after he was inducted into the Major League Baseball Hall of Fame in 2014, and six years after his Saint Louis Cardinals Hall of Fame induction in 2016. I asked Torre in 2024, during my research for this book, if the Braves somehow withheld his Braves Hall of Fame induction until they won their 2021 World Series championship because he took two World Series championships away from them with the Yankees, he gave the question no oxygen to ignite any negativity.

"I just go about my business; I am not sure what took the Braves so long. But when the team reached out to me about it, I never hesitated to do it, and I told them I would be there," said Torre.

But much like everything else, plans changed as COVID-19 spread across the world in 2020. "The date was put off a year when COVID hit. I finally went down there, and it was cool to reunite with them," explained Torre.

For Torre and the Braves, a dynasty may have been disrupted in 1985. But for the Braves and Torre, it all worked out during the long, serendipitous roller-coaster journey, with lots of winning, some losing, and setting marks to be cherished along the way in baseball history.

NOTES

CHAPTER 2: THE ABYSS

Pythagorean winning percentage is an estimate of a team's winning percentage given their runs scored and runs allowed (*Baseball-Reference* FAQs - Sports-Reference.com)

CHAPTER 3: THE RISE

"*I couldn't be happier*": Pluto, Terry, "Barker Is Traded to Braves," *Cleveland Plain Dealer*, September 29, 1983.

CHAPTER 4: ROLLER COASTER GOING UP

"*We do not train that kind of baseball*" : Associated Press, "Atlanta Luckiest in No. 13," *Spartanburg Herald-Journal*, April 22, 1982.

"*I think we're capable, yes*": *The Sporting News* archives, "Braves Optimism," March 1, 1982.

"*He [Bob Watson] made the difference*" : Tucker, Tim, "Watson Making a Difference," *The Sporting News*, May 24, 1982.

"*Just look at him over there*": Reilly, Rick, "So Good, He's Scary," *Sports Illustrated*, June 3, 1985.

"*MLB All-Decade Team*": Schoenfield, David, "Who Made Our Squad of Baseball's Best from 2010 to 2019?" *ESPN*, December 26, 2019.

"*Should have his or her voting rights revoked*": Ryan, Bob, X, formerly known as Twitter, January 22, 2025.

"*I've been coming to the Hall of Fame*": Leahy, Sean, "Who Didn't for Ichiro?" *Yahoo Sports*, January 23, 2025.

CHAPTER 5: ROLLER COASTER GOING DOWN

"If we're nine games ahead": Staff, "N.L. West Races," *Atlanta Journal*, August 3, 1982.

"Everybody's making too big a deal about this" : Staff, "Braves Chase," *Pensacola News-Journal*, August 1, 1982.

"I don't think we can find a silver lining in this" : Staff, "Giants Still in Race," *San Francisco Examiner*, July 31, 1982.

"Our starting pitchers have to be more consistent" : Staff, "Braves Skid," *The Sporting News*, August 16, 1982.

"I can only speak for myself" : Staff, "Braves Skid," *The Sporting News*, August 16, 1982.

"There's a big radio, and the merengue music was real loud" : Lidz, Frank, "Wild and Crazy Hombres," *Sports Illustrated*, January 8, 1990.

"My whole idea is to throw the ball over the plate" : Anderson, Dave, "George Bamberger, the Brewers Ph.D. in Pitching" *New York Times*, March 8, 1979.

"It was Pascual Perez getting lost" : Tucker, Tim, "Perez Turned Braves Around on I-285," *Atlanta Constitution*, August 29, 1982.

CHAPTER 6: THE CHASE

"The pitching still worries me" : Staff, "N.L West Battle," *The Sporting News*, Monday, September 20, 1982.

"I have nothing personal against anyone on the Dodgers" : Peters, Nick, "Giants End Dodgers Playoff Hopes," *Gannett News Service*, printed *Salinas Californian*, October 4, 1982.

"It was getting stale with the Dodgers around every year" : Staff, "Giants Oust Dodgers, Braves Take Crown," *The Sporting News*, October 4, 1982.

"Why did the chicken cross the road" : WTBS, "It's a Long Way to October," *The 1982 Braves*, 1983 WTBS.

"We've been at death's door a couple of times this year" : "What a Way to Win It," AP Article, *Anderson Independent-Mail*, October 4, 1982.

CHAPTER 7: THE 1982 PLAYOFFS

"There is no emotion for me" : Strother, Shelby, "Gibson Still Prideful, Bitter," *St. Petersburg Times*, October 10, 1982.

"Because of my career in St. Louis" : Smith, Paul, "Torre and Gibson Bravely Return to St. Louis," *Tallahassee Democrat*, October 6, 1982.

"I was disappointed" : Staff, "Niekro Rained Out," *The Sporting News*, October 11, 1982.

"Whitey came to me" : AP Wire, "Cards Skipper Claims Rain Advantage," *Bremerton Sun*, October 7, 1982.

"You're always excited about pitching": Bisher, Furman, "Phil Niekro: Hungry at 43," *The Sporting News*, October 11, 1982.

"That's great, but we didn't win" : Staff, "Braves Ace Knuckleballer Still Ready to Take the Mound," *The Stuart News*, October 10, 1982.

"I was looking at Oberkfell or Hernandez" : Staff, "Torre Decides Against Playing by the Book, and Pays," AP, *The Dayton Daily News*, October 11, 1982.

"Good pitching beats good hitting every time": Staff, "Cards, Brewers in World Series," *The Leaf-Chronicle*, October 11, 1982.

CHAPTER 8: 1983 AS THE FAVORITES

"I think it was more a tribute to how our team did" : AP Staff, "Braves' Murphy Wins N.L. MVP," AP, *York Daily Record*, November 18, 1982.

"It's very satisfactory and kind of funny" : AP Staff, "Braves' Joe Torre Wins N.L. Manager of the Year," AP, *York Daily Record*, October 28, 1982.

"The biggest injustice of my life": Staff, "Non-Starter Royster Mad" *The Reporter, Fond du Lac, Wisconsin: Gannett Media Corp,* March 24, 1983.

"I told Jerry, maybe I am selfish" : Staff, "Non-Starter Royster Mad," *The Reporter, Fond du Lac, Wisconsin: Gannett Media Corp,* March 24, 1983.

"It's a lot like a lap time at the Indianapolis 500" : Staff, "Will The All-Star Break Hurt or Hinder Red-Hot Braves?" AP, *Leaf Chronicle*, July 6, 1983.

CHAPTER 9: THE IMPATIENCE OF THE 1984 OFFSEASON

"It wasn't just manager Joe Torre, or pitching coach Bob Gibson" : "Niekro May Be on His Way Out for Braves," *Lebanon Daily News,* October 6, 1983.

"I wasn't about to go to spring training" : Staff, "Phil Niekro Nixes Atlanta's Options," *The Dayton Daily News,* October 8, 1983.

"We were disappointed we didn't win the division" : Chris Mortenson, "Turner Backs Torre on Niekro Criticisms," *Atlanta Constitution,* October 14, 1983.

"I have no control over such things" : Richman, Milton. "Braves Still Contenders Says Torre," *Atlanta Daily World,* February 5, 1984.

"I don't want anyone to think we're going to let it go": AP Staff, "Braves Scuffle Before Exhibition Game," AP, *Public Opinion,* March 9, 1984.

CHAPTER 10: THE BRAVES TURN LEFT

"To me, Bruce is the best there ever was" : Fink, David, "Herzog Losing Sutter," *Pittsburgh Post-Gazette,* March 6, 1985.

CHAPTER 11: IT HAD TO HAPPEN

"You have fun this winter" : Tucker, Tim, "WORLD SERIES BRAVES VS. YANKEES the Torre Story Shows Tough City Has a Heart." *The Atlanta Constitution,* October 28, 1996.

BIBLIOGRAPHY

Anderson, Dave, "George Bamberger, the Brewers Ph.D. in Pitching," *New York Times*, March 8, 1979.
AP Wire, "Braves Ace Knuckleballer Still Ready to Take the Mound," *Stuart News*, October 10, 1982.
AP Wire, "Cards Skipper Claims Rain Advantage," *Bremerton Sun*, October 7, 1982.
"The Atlanta Braves Lost Veteran Pitcher Donnie Moore Thursday," *UPI Archives*, January 25, 1985.
"Atlanta Luckiest in No. 13," *Spartanburg Herald-Journal*, Associated Press, April 22, 1982.
Bisher, Furman, "Phil Niekro: Hungry at 43," *The Sporting News*, October 11, 1982.
"Braves Chase," *Pensacola News-Journal*, August 1, 1982.
"Braves' Joe Torre Wins N.L. Manager of the Year," *York Daily Record*, October 28, 1982.
"Braves' Murphy Wins N.L. MVP," *York Daily Record*, November 18, 1982.
"Braves Optimism" *Sporting News* archives, March 1, 1982.
"Braves Scuffle Before Exhibition Game," *Public Opinion*, March 9, 1984.
"Braves Skid," *The Sporting News*, August 16, 1982.
"Cards, Brewers in World Series," *Leaf Chronicle*," October 11, 1982.
"Giants Oust Dodgers, Braves Take Crown," *The Sporting News*, October 4, 1982.
"Herzog Losing Sutter," *Pittsburgh Post-Gazette*, March 6, 1985.
"It's a Long Way to October," *The 1982 Braves*, 1983 WTBS.
Leahy, Sean, "Who Didn't Vote for Ichiro?" *Yahoo Sports*, January 23, 2025.
Lidz, Frank, "Wild and Crazy Hombres," *Sports Illustrated*, January 8, 1990.
"Niekro Getting Hot," *The Sporting News*, September 13, 1982,
"Niekro May Be on His Way Out for Braves," *Lebanon Daily News*, October 6, 1983.
"Niekro Rained Out," *The Sporting News*, October 11, 1982.
"N.L West Battle," *The Sporting News*, Monday, September 20, 1982.
"Non-Starter Royster Mad" *Fond du Lac (Wisconsin) Reporter*, March 24, 1983.
Peters, Nick, "Giants End Dodgers Playoff Hopes," *Salinas Californian*, October 4, 1982.
"Phil Niekro Nixes Atlanta's Options," *Dayton Daily News*, October 8, 1983.
Pluto, Terry, "Barker Is Traded to Braves," *Cleveland Plain Dealer*, September 29, 1983.
Reilly, Rick, "So Good, He's Scary," *Sports Illustrated*, June 3, 1985.
Report, Staff, "Giants Still in Race," *San Francisco Examiner*, July 31, 1982.
Richman, Milton. "Braves Still Contenders Says Torre." *Atlanta Daily World*, Feb 5, 1984.
Ryan, Bob, "Whoever Did Not Vote for Ichiro Suzuki," X (formerly known as Twitter), January 22, 2025.
Schoenfield, David, "MLB All-Decade Team: Who Made Our Squad of Baseball's Best from 2010 to 2019?" *ESPN*, December 26, 2019.
Smith, Paul, "Torre and Gibson Bravely Return to St. Louis," *Tallahassee Democrat*, October, 6, 1982.

Staff, "N.L. West Races," *Atlanta Journal*, August 3, 1982.
Strother, Shelby, "Gibson Still Prideful, Bitter," *St. Petersburg Times*, October 10, 1982.
"Torre Decides Against Playing by the Book, and Pays," *Dayton Daily News*, October 11, 1982.
Tucker, Tim, "Perez Turned Braves Around on I-285," *Atlanta Constitution*, August 29, 1982.
Tucker, Tim, "Watson Making a Difference," *Sporting News*, May 24, 1982.
Tucker, Tim. "World Series Braves vs. Yankees: The Torre Story Shows Tough City Has a Heart." *Atlanta Constitution*, October 28, 1996.
"Turner Backs Torre on Niekro Criticisms," *Atlanta Constitution*, October 9, 1983.
"What a Way to Win It," *Anderson (South Carolina) Independent-Mail*, October 4, 1982.
"Will the All-Star Break Hurt of Hinder Red-Hot Braves?" *Leaf Chronicle*, July 6, 1983.

INDEX

Aaron, Hank 1, 11, 16, 19, 32, 35, 39, 59, 102, 145
Aaron, Tommie 146
Adcock, Joe 11
Alou, Felipe 15–16
Alou, Matty 16
Andujar, Joaquin 53, 127, 133–4, 139–41

Barker, Len 23–4, 27, 30, 157, 161–2, 183, 187
Bartholomay, William 12
Bedrosian, Steve 25–6, 32, 47, 71, 73–4, 78, 83, 91, 110–11, 131, 142, 148, 153
Behenna, Rick 24, 31, 162
Bench, Johnny 41, 51, 55, 66–7, 121–2, 150
Benedict, Bruce 26, 42, 45–6, 51, 64–5, 82–3, 86, 100, 116, 130, 134, 149
Berenyi, Bruce 43
Berra, Dale 44, 46, 60
Biittner, Larry 42
Boggs, Tommy 41, 60, 109–10, 132–3, 162
Bonds, Barry 32
Bonnell, Barry 28
Bristol, Dave 22
Butler, Brett 24, 26, 27, 30–1, 40, 42–3, 50, 54, 97, 99–100, 106, 111, 137–8, 149, 157

Camp, Rick 27–8, 32, 40, 45, 47, 74, 83, 96–7, 106, 109, 113, 119–20, 140, 149
Carty, Rico 16
Chambliss, Chris 28, 37, 40–2, 44, 46, 50, 51, 55, 56, 63, 66, 72, 78, 82, 97, 90, 100, 111, 113, 116, 117–18, 126–7, 136, 140–3, 149, 173
Cloninger, Tony 16

Cole, Jesse 21
Concepcion, Dave 41–2
Cowley, Joe 46, 73–4, 82
Cox, Bobby 38, 64, 169–72, 174–5, 178–80
Crandall, Del 11
Cruz, Jose 50

Eichelberger, Juan 40

Garber, Gene 29, 41, 45, 47, 49, 53, 72, 74, 76–8, 82–3, 100, 104–5, 111–12, 138, 136–7, 142, 149
Garcia, Damaso 32
Gehrig, Lou 2
Glavine, Tom 37, 163, 169–71, 180
Gomez, Luis 28

Henderson, Dave 35
Hernandez, Keith 49, 131, 134–5, 137–8, 140, 185
Horner, Bob 1, 2, 22, 29–30, 32, 37, 40–1, 45–8, 50–1, 53, 55–6, 58, 63, 71–6, 79, 82, 86, 96, 97, 99–100, 106–8, 119, 147–50, 154, 156, 159–63, 164, 180
Hubbard, Glenn 30, 40–6, 50, 56, 78, 81–3, 100, 110–11, 135–7, 130, 155, 141, 147, 149
Hume, Tom 42–3

Jackson, Bo 8
Jacoby, Brook 24, 30, 31, 157, 162
Jenkins, Ferguson 46
Johnson, Randy 52
Johnstone, Jay 53
Jones, Chipper 35, 169, 172, 179–80
Jones, Mack 16

Kern, Jim 42
Kimbrel Craig 29
Knepper, Bob 50–1
Knight, Ray 50
Kuhn, Bowie 17–18, 21, 22

Leal, Luis 32
Linares, Rufino 42, 50–1, 81, 93
Lurie, Bob 21–2
Lynn, Fred 34

Mack, Connie 22
McCormick, Mike 16
McLaughlin, Joey 28
McMurtry, Craig 31–2, 149, 151–3, 161, 164
McReynolds, Larry 36, 121
McWilliams, Larry 44, 47, 52
Mahler, Rick 25, 31, 40–2, 74, 80, 85–6, 107–8, 142
Mantle, Mickey 2, 59
Maris, Roger 2
Mathews, Eddie 11, 15
Matthews, Gary 97
Messersmith, Andy 21
Meyer, Urban 52
Moffitt, Randy 51
Moore, Donnie 33–5, 120, 131, 141
Moreno, Omar 44–5, 54, 56
Moskau, Paul 45
Mullen, John 34, 51, 150, 159, 169, 172, 179
Murphy, Dale 1–2, 25–6, 35, 37, 42, 45–50, 53–5, 58–68, 71–4, 79, 81–2, 85–6, 93–4, 96–7, 100, 103, 106, 110–11, 113, 118–19, 124, 130, 136, 138, 140–1, 143, 145–7, 149, 151, 153–6, 170–3, 179–80

Niekro, Joe 50, 101, 102, 103, 132, 150
Niekro, Phil 11, 29, 35, 37, 40, 44, 49, 50, 53, 65, 72, 74, 77, 78, 87, 89, 90, 100–104, 113, 107, 112, 115, 119, 126, 127, 131–4, 138–9, 142, 147, 149–52, 159, 164, 171, 180

Parker, Dave 44–5
Perez, Pascual 32, 36, 52, 74–6, 85, 90, 91, 99, 104, 108, 117, 119, 129–31, 140–2, 149, 152–3, 161, 163
Perini, Lou 12
Pocoraba, Biff 40, 42, 49, 51, 64, 93, 138
Price, Joe 42

Quisenberry, Dan 34, 169

Ramirez, Rafael 37, 40–5, 75, 79, 81, 82, 93, 96, 100, 111–13, 117, 130, 134, 135, 149
Ray, Johnny 44
Rios, Carlos 52
Ripken, Cal 25, 60
Rockett, Pat 28, 110
Rose, Pete 29, 96, 109
Royster, Jerry 51, 79, 93, 96, 99, 100, 103, 108, 110–12, 118, 135–6, 149–50
Ruth, Babe 1, 2, 6–8, 19, 59
Ruthven, Dick 29

Sanders, Deion 8
Scurry, Rod 45–6
Seaver, Tom 41, 86, 92, 104, 150
Selig, Bud 18
Shanahan, Bill 21
Shirley, Bob 42
Sinatro, Matt 42–3, 93, 111, 121
Smith, Pete 25
Smith, Zane 52
Smoltz, John 29, 36–7, 169, 171, 175, 177, 180
Solomon, Eddie 44–5
Soto, Mario 41–3
Spahn, Warren 11
Steinbrenner, George 21, 169, 172, 174
Strawberry, Darryl 32
Sutter, Bruce 33–4, 37, 52, 136–8, 141, 142, 168–9

Tekulve, Kent 46
Thompson, Jason 45

Thompson, Milt 25
Thon, Dickie 49, 54
Thorpe, Jim 6, 8
Torre, Joe 2–3, 11, 15–16, 30, 36, 38–9, 42–4, 46, 48–51, 53–4, 56, 58, 67–8, 71, 74, 75, 77, 81, 82, 84–5, 87, 89, 91, 93–4, 97, 100–1, 106–10, 112–13, 116, 117, 121, 124–6, 128–9, 131–3, 137–8, 140–3, 145, 147–50, 152, 155, 159–62, 164, 167
Turner, Ted 18–22, 29, 33, 39, 43, 70–1, 81, 88, 120–1, 123, 143, 146–7, 150, 159–61, 167–9, 171, 174, 176, 179, 181

Veeck, Bill 21
Virdon, Bill 50
Virgil, Ozzie 25

Walk, Bob 72, 75, 79–80
Washington, Claudell 41–3, 45–8, 50, 55, 58, 72, 75–8, 93–4, 96, 115–16, 127, 130, 133–5, 141, 149, 161
Watson, Bob 37, 46–48, 100, 106, 110–11, 118, 149, 173
Whisenton, Larry 51, 78, 93

Young, Cy 6–8, 60

ABOUT THE AUTHOR

Patrick Montgomery is an award-winning writer. His first book, *The Baseball Miracle of the Splendid 6*, garnered first place for Sports Book at the 2022 Speak Up Talk Radio Firebird Book Awards and was a winner in the 2022 Hollywood Book Festival. His most recent book, published by Rowman & Littlefield in 2023, *Baseball's Great Expectations: Candid Stories of Ballplayers Who Didn't Live Up to the Hype*, earned a Booklist Starred Review and a Booklist Top-10 Book on Sports 2024.

Montgomery is a baseball historian, geek, and student of the game, including membership in the premier baseball research group, the Society for American Baseball Research (SABR). Montgomery's unique and interesting background includes being a retired Coast Guard officer, an actor, and the husband of a New Jersey girl. His professional background includes being a federal, state, and local public affairs officer, a US Coast Guard equal rights and diversity liaison to the Department of Defense, and Department of Homeland Security (DHS) tribal liason. Highlights and lowlights of Montgomery's career include on-site media officer duties for the Deepwater Horizon oil spill, Miracle on the Hudson, US Airways Flight 1549, various hurricanes, and DHS National Special Security Events including Republican and Democratic conventions as well as the Olympics.

Patrick Montgomery's most recent book
Baseball's Great Expectations: Candid Stories of Ballplayers Who Didn't Live Up to the Hype (Rowman & Littlefield, 2023).

Drawing from his extensive interviews with the players, family members, general managers, executives, scouts, and more, Montgomery shines a fresh light on these players and provides a candid perspective on the major leagues. Players reflect on their careers, what went wrong, how they feel about baseball now that their playing days are over, and, for many of them, how they have found new purpose in their lives.

[It's] Montgomery's journalistic eye for distilling the humanity behind the unfulfilled athletic potential that makes this a real home run.
—*Booklist*, Starred Review • A *Booklist* Top 10 Book on Sports 2024

The author is happy to hear your thoughts!
ptmontgomerybooks@gmail.com
Twitter: @MontgomeryBook
Twitter: @Tdmonty
https//www.amazon.com/author/patrickmontgomery